Key Persons in the Nursery

Building relationships for quality provision

Peter Elfer
Elinor Goldschmied
Dorothy Selleck

David Fulton Publishers Ltd
The Chiswick Centre, 414 Chiswick High Road, London W4 5TF

www.fultonpublishers.co.uk

First published in Great Britain in 2003 by David Fulton Publishers
10 9 8 7 6 5 4 3

David Fulton Publishers is a division of Granada Learning Limited

Note: The right of Peter Elfer, Elinor Goldschmied and Dorothy Selleck to be
identified as the authors of this work has been asserted by them in accordance
with the Copyright, Designs and Patents Act 1988.

Copyright © Peter Elfer, Elinor Goldschmied and Dorothy Selleck 2003

British Library Cataloguing in Publication Data
A catalogue record for this book is available from the British Library.

ISBN 1–84312–079–8
EAN 978-1-84312-079-7

Typeset by FiSH Books, London
Printed and bound in Great Britain

Contents

Acknowledgements   v

Introduction   vi

1   Parenting and working, children and nursery   1
Public policy and private choices   1
What counts in quality?   3
Nursery: a home from home?   5
Nursery: not a substitute home but a place to be different   7
Relationship is key: the theory   9
Relationship is key: a child's perspective   14

2   What is the key person approach?   18
The benefits of a key person approach   18
Why 'key person' and not 'key worker'?   19
The key person approach for babies and young children   19
The key person approach for parents, particularly mothers   23
The key person approach for the key person   26
The key person approach for the nursery   27

3   A strategy for implementation   29
Values, principles, research evidence and ... time!   30
Building an approach, rather than a system   31
Practical realities   34
    Home visits and establishing a partnership   34
    Building a key group   35
    Aiding professional growth   46
    The key person approach: essential elements of the role   47
    Employers supporting the key person approach   49

Observing, noticing and not noticing   50
Sharing and not sharing information   51
Physical contact and closeness, abuse and boundaries   53
Mentoring and supervision   55

4   The key person approach: what would you look for?   **60**
Thinking about the details of the key person approach   60

References and further reading   **76**

Index   **81**

Acknowledgements

THE INSPIRATION FOR THE key person approach came from Elinor Goldschmied, an internationally renowned trainer and early years consultant. This book, and her part in it, is a loving celebration of her work. Elinor has supported many of us on our quest for understanding the meaning of quality in relation to work with babies and young children.

Our evolving understanding over the years of the subtleties of the interactions between parents, children and staff in the 'world of nursery', was only able to get off the ground because so many nursery managers and staff were open to us spending time observing what went on in their nurseries.

We want to pay tribute to their professional openness and generosity; and to parents, who seemed to be speaking very much from the heart. We also thank Janice Baker of Avranches Nursery, Jersey; Bernadette Duffy of Thomas Coram Early Years Centre; Ruth Forbes of Jigsaw Nurseries; Jacqui Gibb of 197; Julien Grenier of Woodlands Park Nursery Centre; and Mary West, Miranda Martin and everyone working in the under-threes unit at the Randolph Beresford Early Years Centre, who have talked through the practicalities of making the key person approach work.

But, above all, it is the babies and young children who, when we found ways to listen carefully enough, taught us most about what matters in nurseries, often long before they could talk.

Introduction

CHILDREN BEGIN THEIR LIVES secure in the safety of laps, families and nurseries. But however loved and cherished children are, childhood includes times and events that may be difficult or painful to cope with. Alongside the magic and fun, children might experience sadness and anxiety – even terror and bereavement.

Wide-eyed toddlers who *are* whirring aeroplanes above adults' heads – and who come crashing down onto soft sofas – are rehearsing treacheries and triumphs. This 'playing up' and 'playing it out' is the stuff of growing up. Powerful thinkers, lovers and learners begin in families and often go on to nurseries to live out and learn these things too.

We believe that what babies and young children experience in the beginning in families – and in nurseries – makes a difference. Adults help children manage the emotional roller-coaster that life can be. Parents do this for their children as part of day-to-day parenting, even when the incessant demands can threaten to overwhelm them. The paradox of parenting is that it is so ordinary and so special at the same time.

In *Key Persons in the Nursery* we suggest that even the youngest children need special kinds of relationships when they are cared for away from their parents, to 'set them up' for life. We introduce and argue the case for a *key person approach* and describe the benefits for everyone involved. We explain how any nursery can develop such an approach, whereby one or two adults in the nursery, while never taking over from parents, connect with what parents would ordinarily do: being special for the children, helping them manage throughout the day, thinking about them, getting to know them well, and sometimes worrying about them too – all of which help a child to make a strong link between home and nursery. We have called the person who bears that role the child's *key person*. The organisational set-up within the setting that makes it all happen is the *key person approach*.

Peter Elfer, Elinor Goldschmied and Dorothy Selleck
May 2003

Parenting and working, children and nursery

Public policy and private choices

> Parents will not be given a legal right to work flexible hours but will have a right to request it, the government said yesterday as details of its taskforce to improve access to family-friendly working were published.
>
> *(Guardian*, 29 June 2001)

The taskforce had a tricky job, trying to help parents piece together the complicated jigsaw of being at home and being at work. The practicalities of finding a job and a nursery where the hours fit together, never mind the journeys, is not straightforward. If parents also have school-age children, the logistics are worse. Then there are holidays, late starts on days following holidays and INSET days. Covering for children's illnesses hardly bears thinking about.

But achieving a balance of family life, work and nursery involves much more than the fitting of work around nursery hours – or nursery around working hours. There are emotional transactions to be negotiated: balancing personal needs and children's needs, time at home and additional income, being a 'good' employee and being a 'good enough' parent (Winnicott 1988). Striking these balances has to be done in a society that seems to be continually changing its policies and attitudes to earning and parenting. Public policy has certainly come a long way in the last 50 years.

While the present Labour government seems to want to encourage both women and men to work outside the home, this has certainly not always been the case. At the close of the Second World War, the Ministry of Health could not have been more explicit:

> In the interests of the health and development of the child ... the right policy to pursue would be positively to discourage mothers of children under two from going out to work.
>
> (Ministry of Health and Ministry of Education 1945: 1)

Since 1945, the demand for greater fairness between women and men, equality of opportunity, changing family needs, and the growth of the economy have combined to gradually enable a change of message about how our youngest children are cared for. The 1998 National Childcare Strategy (DfEE 1998) incorporates childcare tax credits, aimed squarely at helping women with young children access the labour market. Improvements in parental-leave arrangements and family-friendly working practices are all supposed to help families achieve life balances.

Public policy impacts directly on the personal choices parents make because it influences the very supply of nursery places, their cost and their quality. But public attitudes have a strong impact too. The roles women and men, mothers and fathers, take at home and at work, as portrayed in films, TV, and in the media, also shape the life balances that families strike. At one time a father who did not work outside the home was seen as irresponsible – but so too was a mother who did. Equally, women who did not work outside the home were bored or boring. They seemed blamed and shamed whatever they did.

Many parents, particularly mothers, still seem deeply anxious about whether the care of children outside the family home, however good it is, can be good enough. Yet the main conclusion of researchers is that good-quality services are not harmful (Rutter 1995; Schaffer 1998). More than this though, good-quality childcare can bring positive benefits: both parents are able to work and the family enjoys a better standard of living. And children may end up with the best of both worlds – the love and uniqueness of private family life, and being part of a nursery community of adults and other children.

Alongside changes in public policy, more flexibility and less blame in cultural attitudes about male and female roles seems to have freed up the choices that people make about sharing child-rearing, earning, and running a home. How 'free' such choices feel to those who make them and how well they work in practice depends on many factors, not least how much parents earn and how much they have to pay for nursery care. The flexibility of working hours and nursery hours is another key factor. Alongside these essential practicalities, we believe there are two other critical factors that determine the impact of nursery care on the daily lives of children, parents and nursery staff.

The first is the *quality* of the nursery and the second is how the two worlds of home and nursery can be 'joined up'. We believe the key to both these factors converges in the idea of the key person approach.

What counts in quality? ✳

'Quality' is a slippery concept. It is universally used – 'quality education', 'quality standards' – as if everyone shares the same understanding of what it means in practice. But just as different drivers will want different things from a car (size, style, reliability, etc.) different parents will give different priorities to different aspects of a nursery (location, programme of activities, approach of the manager, facilities and equipment, and so forth).

When asked what they think is most important, a majority of parents and nursery workers list practical things first – safety, hygiene, quality of the food and sufficient staff numbers. But they also say that while these are essential, they are not the whole story. What matters most, once the practicalities are in place, are the staff: what they do and how they interact with the children.

This strong parental and practitioner consensus is supported by research:

> Children do need sensitive and responsive adults to care for them. These adults may be parents, grandparents, nursery workers or childminders. Children do need stable and consistent care. Environments which do not provide these experiences for children, whether home or childcare, are likely to increase the risk of poorer outcomes.
>
> (Mooney and Munton 1997: 25)

Penelope Leach (1997: 218), in direct advice to parents, emphasises the same central point:

> Day care can only be as good for your child as the people who do the caring, so look first at staff training and/or experience, support and supervision; your baby needs intimate, consistent, individual care.

To this extent, researchers and writers, practitioners and parents seem to broadly agree about what counts in judging quality. However, when Mooney and Munton speak of 'consistency', what do they mean – and how much 'consistency' is needed? And when Leach speaks of 'individual' care, does this mean only one person should be assigned to each child?

Consistency partly means that the majority of staff working in a nursery this month will still be there, working together, next month. It refers to staff turnover and the importance of this being low. But it also refers to a more detailed consistency during each day with regard to how many different people hold and care for each child. For example, if a baby has five nappy changes in a day, and a different person carries out each one, is that sufficiently 'consistent'? If six different people give a toddler her lunch – one washing face and hands, another sitting her in her high chair, a third spooning in the first course, a fourth feeding her pudding, a fifth also taking a turn with the spoon and a sixth wiping her face and hands before getting her down at the end – is that sufficiently consistent?

These issues of who does what with each child in nursery, the number of different people that should be involved and the details of how they interact, are all very practical questions that lie at the heart of big debate about quality. But they raise an even bigger question about the kind of place a nursery should, ideally, be.

Most people, watching the interaction between a baby and parent figure, are moved by the intensity of their mutual love affair. While the baby's adoration, delight and playfulness can seem to quickly collapse into sadness or even despair, there is no escaping the intense passion and special nature of these interactions. This is simply how babies are!

This baby is curious, involved and sharing the preoccupations and activities of the day with his significant adults at home. He is being held firmly and in a position where he can see and scrutinise new experiences and sensations, but is still in close contact with the familiar sensations of smell, voice and body temperature of his father. Ben is learning in a safe and supported lap, but is free to 'read' and explore the paper.

But why? Is this intense interaction, like any other love affair, purely for its own sake, unique and irreplaceable, a wonderful part of the human condition? Or does it also have a purpose? Is this interaction, in the form it takes, present for a reason? Does it matter for the child's healthy development?

In relation to nurseries, we can ask these questions in another way. We know that monomatry (infants being cared for by one mother figure) is not a precondition for healthy human development (McGurk *et al.* 1993). But do nurseries need to be places where *some* features of the relationship with mothers and fathers are provided for each child? These features might include coming to know the child very well, showing the child spontaneity, immediacy and delight in interactions, and the ability to be involved in an intense relationship without being overwhelmed by it.

[handwritten margin note: more than one mother?]

We are not suggesting that nursery relationships can be the same as home relationships, but we do ask whether some aspects of the optimal parental relationship need to be replicated in nursery. Are nurseries best understood as an extension of home, where children meet a wider range of adults and children but are still mainly cared for by a small number of people, in relationships that replicate some aspects of home relationships? The key person approach is designed to support this model of nursery practice.

Or is nursery better understood in a quite different way? The unique nature of home relationships and their importance to healthy development are understood and acknowledged. However, there is no need to attempt to reproduce any of the attributes of these home relationships in nursery. Nursery is an opportunity for children, from the earliest age, to experience and participate in a network of relationships, with other children as well as adults, which are much broader and more open than within a family. The key person approach would then be completely unnecessary and restrictive.

Nursery: a home from home?

Is the job of a nursery worker, in a 'good-quality' nursery, to be rather like a loving parent? Nursery workers sometimes speak as if the role is like that of a parent although they are often careful to say it is *not the same* as a parent. Kiva, an experienced nursery practitioner working in a local authority nursery in a rural area speaks first:

> *'I don't know if this is going to sound unprofessional – it's almost like being another mother, especially for little Linda. Things a mother would do like cuddles and making them feel secure. It's love, it's not what you learn in college but it is LOVE. Of course they're not your babies but . . . oh, I don't know, it's really hard . . .'*

(Elfer, forthcoming)

Nigella works in a private nursery in an inner city:

> '…while we're taking on a part of the parent's role of parent for them, while they're here and they get that love at home so they should expect to get it here – all the little kisses and the cuddles and everything else that they get at home they have to have here. It's just part of looking after them, part of their play routine.
>
> I think it must be (a different sort of love from parental love) yes, I think it must be. It's just the fact that it's all part of the job, even if you have a terrible day with them and they've cried and not been very happy, you've still got to think well, yes, this child's important and special and you just have to do it.'

> (Ibid.)

These two nursery workers seem to be emphasising the similarity of a part of their work to that of being a parent. *But similarity does not mean the same.* In their different ways, they both make it plain that their role is a professional one, not a parental one, and part of this professional role is to maintain that clear distinction.

In the following extract, a nursery worker and nursery manager speak positively of the benefits of close relationships and why they can be difficult in practice:

> Louise: 'On Tuesday this week, Tina was on her way to work in the Baby Unit, when she had a car accident. She wasn't badly hurt, although the car was a write-off, but she'll be off for a couple of days. Joseph is only just one and he's so linked himself to Tina. He just wouldn't settle when he arrived this morning and although I tried to cuddle him, he just went all stiff – I know he just wanted Tina, not me. It was horrible for him and it's a horrible feeling too when they don't want you. You have got to work hard in nursery to get the children to be used to all the staff and to be able to manage with all the members of the team. You can see the problem if they get too attached to one person.'

> Brenda: 'It's a bit the same with Adam. I am not permanently in any of the three baby rooms because, as manager, I "float". But Adam, who is nearly two, is so insistent that I somehow belong to him and that he can be on my lap whenever I go into the room. I've always got a group of three or four of them round me but he just pushes his way on and I have to put him off because my lap is just not big enough for them all and it's not fair to let just one… But he makes such a fuss – he's lovely but it really is quite a lot of trouble to handle that every time I go into that room. Louise is right, we do need to work as a team and they do need to be able to manage with each member of the team otherwise it's not really fair to them.'

> (Ibid.)

These workers seem to be making the case that, in an ideal world, close relationships with particular members of staff are important and valuable but, because it is so difficult to achieve them reliably, it is better to work together providing team rather than individual care.

Staff, in general, seem very sensitive to these issues of fairness, rivalry and the dangers of developing preferences. They are usually very aware that being in a professional role that comes close to a parental one will sometimes make parents fearful that they are going to be replaced. Samantha's mother expresses this fearfulness, almost as an aside, as she talks about how she and her husband came to choose a nursery, rather than a childminder for their daughter:

> 'Why did we choose nursery for Samantha? The opportunity for her to mix with other children of similar age was important to both of us. But if I'm honest, I think I probably was a bit nervous about her making a very close relationship with a childminder and coming to feel a bit redundant. In that sense a nursery did seem safer – I could say to myself, well it's just the same really as her going to school, except she is starting earlier.'

> (Ibid.)

Nursery practitioners surely meet this kind of fearfulness, expressed in many different forms and at many different times. Who would not be extremely wary of the dangers of allowing, or even unwittingly encouraging, children to blur the boundaries between who is Mummy and Daddy and who is a special adult at nursery?

Louise refers to how difficult Joseph found it not to be able to have the member of staff he most wanted to greet him. She also makes plain that it can then be very difficult for the member of staff who *is* there. Brenda speaks of treating each child the same. If they cannot all be on her lap all of the time (and of course they cannot) then she seems to feel strongly that no child should have sole occupancy of her lap. Nursery cannot be a home from home in this way.

Nursery: not a substitute home but a place to be different

Other writers have argued that nursery should not, even ideally, be like home. Dahlberg *et al.* (1999), for instance, radically analyse the place in society of what they call the 'Early Childhood Institution'. We haven't the space here to do justice to the depth of their full discussion but, from the point of view of relationships *within* nursery, the following quotations capture the essence of their case against emotional closeness and intimacy:

> It is not to be understood as a substitute home. Young children – both under three and over three years of age – are seen as able to manage, and indeed to desire and thrive on relationships with small groups of other children and adults, without risking either their own well-being or their relationship with their parents. Not only is there no need to try in some way to provide a substitute home, but the benefit from attending an early childhood institution comes from it not being a home. It offers something quite different, but quite complementary, so the child gets, so to speak, the best of two environments.

> (Ibid.: 81)

This message is also clear. The 'Early Childhood Institution' is seen as an opportunity for the child to experience quite different relationships with adults and other children than experienced at home. To seek to make the nursery like home is to deny the child that opportunity.

The writers go on:

> If we approach early childhood institutions as forums in civil society, the concept of closeness and intimacy becomes problematic. It can turn public situations and institutions private. As such, it not only creates a 'false closeness' and risks trying to duplicate, necessarily unsuccessfully...it also hinders the ability of the institution to realise its own social life and relationships...
>
> (*Ibid.*: 82)

The argument here is that planning for closeness and intimacy means *over-managing* the relationships of the institution: encouraging some and restricting others. This could be likened to a social gathering where the guests, rather than mixing freely, remain in pairs or small groups so that the possibilities that might be created from a wider group of people mixing together never really develop. The writers go on to introduce an alternative to individual closeness:

> To abandon ideas of intimacy, closeness and cosiness does not leave indifference, callousness or coldness. It does not mean being uncaring. Instead...a contrasting concept to closeness, the concept of **intensity of relationships** implying a complex and dense web or network connecting people, environments and activities which opens up many opportunities for the young child.
>
> (*Ibid.*; emphasis in original)

It is this network of relationships and the importance of each child having access to the whole network and not being confined to individual relationships that sharply distinguishes, in their view, the nursery from the home:

> If the early childhood institution is not understood as a substitute home, then the early childhood worker is also not to be understood as in any way a substitute parent.
>
> (*Ibid.*)

If this sequence of arguments from an academic perspective is combined with the anxieties expressed above by Kiva, Nigella, Louise and Brenda – all experienced practitioners – there seems to be a strong case *against* forming special relationships in nursery. The arguments against the key person approach can be summarised thus:

1 It brings staff too close to a parental role and they risk becoming over-involved.

2 If children get too close to any one member of staff, it is painful for them if that member of staff is not available.

3 It can be threatening for parents who may be jealous of a special relationship between their child and another adult.

4 The key person approach is complex to organise and staff need to work as a team, not as individuals.

5 It undermines the opportunities for children to participate in all nursery-community relationships.

Why then should any nursery go to the trouble of implementing such an approach in the face of all these apparently good reasons not to?

Relationship is key: the theory

We believe these arguments are important ones. The first three are real issues and do involve difficult and painful feelings and the risk of getting it 'wrong', while the fourth is undoubtedly true. In relation to the fifth, there are indeed powerful opportunities to experience participation in the community of the nursery, a microcosm of the wider community in which the nursery is located. This experience is very different from that at home and cannot be had at home with the same richness and variety as at nursery. Parents often say that the opportunity for their child to relate to a much broader group of children and adults is the main reason for choosing nursery.

We believe, however, that the evidence about the nature of human relationships and the longing to form individual attachments, particularly for very young children, is overwhelming. For us, the arguments against individual attachments, to do with feelings and organisation, become challenges to be overcome rather than reasons *not* to develop the key person approach.

Of course, Dahlberg *et al.* do not suggest that the relationships within the dense web of the early childhood institution on which their work is based, therefore lack the features identified by Mooney and Munton (as shown in their extract on page 3 of the present study) as key to healthy staff–child contacts in the nursery and good developmental outcomes for children. Familiarity, attachment and responsiveness are, after all, not identical to intimacy, closeness and cosiness. We do believe, however, that in the UK context, the key person approach is the most effective way of achieving the best possible human relationships in the nursery.

The in-built desire of human infants to be in relationships with others is described very clearly by Schaffer (in Alvarez 1992: 71):

It is increasingly difficult to avoid the conclusion that in some sense, the infant is already prepared for social intercourse...if an infant arrives in the world with a digestive system to cope with food and a breathing apparatus attuned to the air around him, why should he not also be prepared to deal with that essential attribute of his environment, people?

While Alvarez (*ibid.*: 73) suggests that intimate interaction is the very way babies come to be aware of the very existence of other human minds and of their own humanity:

I suggest that those babies being handled all over, talked to, and gazed at are not only being called into awareness of the human world outside themselves, they are being called into awareness that they themselves exist.

Elinor Goldschmied and Sonia Jackson (1994: 37) describe the deep significance of these special relationships in our everyday lives:

Why should it be worth the time and trouble to introduce a key person system in a nursery where this has not been the practice? We have to consider the question not only from the point of view of the child, but also from that of the worker who takes on the emotional responsibility. Thinking of our own relationships as adults may give us some answers.

Most of us have, or would like to have, a special relationship with some person on whom we can rely, a relationship that is significant and precious to us. If we are parted from that person we have ways of preserving continuity even through long separations. We use telephones, letters, photographs, recollections, dreams and fantasies to keep alive the comfort which we derive from such human relationships. When we lose them, we experience sadness and often deep feelings of despair. If we look back we may recall important people in our early lives who, though they are not there in person, give continuity and significance to how we conduct our present lives. Often we seek to repeat and enjoy again the warmth of those relationships in a different form.

Felicity de Zulueta, writing as a psychiatrist and a biologist, puts this argument about the importance of particular relationships in a more academic and general context:

What the attachment behaviour in humans keeps on showing us is how important it is for infants and children to become attached to those who care for them: this is both normal and healthy.

By attending to their infant's psychological and biological needs, parents, and later nursery staff can provide children with a secure attachment which will enable them to develop fruitful long-term relationships and a sense of being valued and loveable. Unfortunately the reverse is also true: by failing to respond in a consistent and sensitive way, psychological damage or trauma may be inflicted upon the child's attachment system and the resultant wounding of their sense of self-esteem and their capacity to relate and tune in to others.

(de Zulueta 2001; personal communication with authors)

Absolutely none of this is to say that babies and very young children cannot thrive in nurseries. Michael Rutter (1995: 559), in a review of all the main evidence, concluded that: 'Most infants who experience good-quality group day care (nursery) with continuity in care-giving show no detectable ill effects.' It is important that the arguments for individual and consistent relationships in nursery are not misunderstood, as indicating that home care is 'best'. The evidence is firm that the quality of relationships *at home and in nursery* both matter.

Other writers, from differing academic branches of psychology, build on what is said by de Zulueta about the pivotal role of individual and special relationships. They give us an insight into the detail of why they matter so much. In the following description, Shore (1997) highlights the significance of relationships to brain development:

Recent research on brain chemistry has found that, starting from birth, the brain is affected by environmental conditions including the kind of nourishment, care, surroundings and stimulations an individual receives. The impact of the environment is dramatic, actually affecting how the brain is wired...During the first three years of life most synapses (connections) are made, and by the age of three, the brains of children are two and a half times more active than the brains of adults. The child's brain at three has twice as many synapses than it will eventually need. Synapses that have been activated many times through early experience tend to become permanent, while those not often used tend to be eliminated.

Environmental conditions matter and there is specific talk here of 'stimulations'. But what kind of 'stimulations' matter? There is no evidence from neuroscience that the 'dense web of relationships' envisaged by Dahlberg *et al.* (1999) provides fewer stimulations and is, therefore, any less able than the key person approach to promote synaptic connections.

But other studies draw out the most important aspects of stimulation in the infant's environment. As Colwyn Trevarthen (1998) suggests:

It is clear from the beginning that children have a driving motivation to become part of a meaningful world. They want to share interests...they like being able to share purposes and actions...Children do need affection and support and protection and so on but they need a lot more than that. They need company which is interested and curious and affectionate...I don't want to underestimate what children can discover for themselves. Children are very good at private research. They can do it very well, but they don't do it if they are discouraged, if they feel unwanted or lonely, then they don't explore.

He argues that the most important features of the environment for the child are the relationships of mutual meaning and understanding that he or she can build – provided the people with whom these relationships are made are 'interested, curious and affectionate'. In principle, why can't such interest, curiosity and affection be shown within the dense web of relationships described by Dahlberg *et al.*?

The answer is that for a baby or very young child, who has not yet acquired the sophisticated tools of verbal communication, the relationship in which interest, curiosity and affection is experienced is a finely tuned one. A baby is delighted and responsive to the minute details of how his mother, or another very familiar adult, holds and talks to him. But an unfamiliar adult's warm and affectionate holding will seem significantly different in detail (smell, facial gestures, physical handling and tone of voice) and can be experienced as completely 'wrong', thus replacing delight with anxiety, stiffness or distress. This seemed to be exactly what Joseph (above) communicated to Louise about her 'inadequacy', despite her warm and affectionate holding of him; she simply was not Tina.

Lisa Miller (1992: 28) describes these crucial details of holding:

> It is quite clear that babies are frightened of falling and that they need the security of feeling nicely pulled together. Inside the womb, they were held from all sides. Now that they are outside, they need moulding and shaping. You can often see a baby who has burrowed into the corner of a cot or crib, as though trying to find a home that will give him shape.
> ...the baby needs not only physical mopping up but lots of mental mopping up. By this I mean that just as surely as he evacuates his bladder or bowels, a baby empties himself of unhappiness. A crying baby is conveying his or her messy misery and needs somebody to receive it. Crying...is communication. It has meaning. But a baby's crying needs an adult's emotional and mental equipment to sort out what it means.

Nursery workers often distinguish types of physical holding they have seen practised, for example babies that are held like 'packages' and babies that are held more closely and sensitively. The importance of being physically held, especially at times of anxiety or distress, must surely be familiar to most human beings. *Who* does this holding cannot be separated from the holding itself. Being held by the 'wrong' person would not have the same effect at all. What makes the right person 'right' is when the holding takes place in the context of a relationship of trust, reliability, familiarity and respect.

Alongside physical holding, Miller refers to mental holding or mental 'mopping up' and the ability of an adult to receive a baby's communications of distress. Anyone who has worked with babies might at first respond to this by thinking that it is almost impossible not to receive a baby's communication of distress – crying can have a powerful and disturbing impact!

But Miller is talking about much more than simply 'hearing the sound' of crying; she is talking about the capacity to think about the possibilities of what it might mean (a full and uncomfortable nappy, a hungry feeling, a sore bottom, being overtired, frightened or missing Mummy). This search for meaning – the preparedness to try and understand what the baby's crying means – seems to be very much an aspect of the 'curiosity' described by Trevarthen above, when he is talking about the kind of adults babies need.

Children are enthusiastic to struggle to make meaning of adult communication and they need to encounter adults who are equally enthusiastic to make meaning of theirs. This is hard work and does not happen automatically. The energy for 'meaning making' comes from a relationship involving commitment, concern, and affection. Can many adults interacting with babies reliably offer such attuned and sensitive responsiveness?

The evidence from these four different branches of psychology – neuroscience, psychiatry, developmental psychology and psychotherapy – represented by Shore, de Zulueta, Trevarthen and Miller, builds an overwhelming case for children's crucial need for relationships with adults. Could these relationships be the dense web described by Dahlberg *et al.* that avoids 'intimacy, closeness and cosiness'? We believe they could *for much older children* who have the physical and emotional resilience to seek out the adults they need and who have a concept of time to hold themselves together, in the 'emotional holding' sense Miller describes, until they get home to familiar adults.

But we cannot see how the 'dense web' can 'collectively' provide the individual tuning with reliability and immediacy upon which babies and toddlers utterly depend and thrive. And why do we feel this is not possible? Why should these special relationships not be offered by a team rather than by mainly one or two particular designated members of staff? Surely six members of a team offering special care and attention to a child is six times better than this being done by just one or two members of staff? At first sight, this seems a strong argument and practitioners who want to argue against the key person principle often use it.

In practice, however, it seems that unless there is specific organisation around the principle of one or two members of staff building special relationships with children, rather than six people building such relationships, *there is an increased risk that these relationships might never occur.* Anybody might change a nappy, greet the child in the morning, help at mealtimes or settle the child to sleep. Such care has been described as 'multiple indiscriminate care'

(Bain and Barnett 1986). This shared team care allows great flexibility of staffing; anybody can do anything, with any child at any time. And although this team care might be carried out with sensitivity and affection, six staff sharing their care equally between perhaps 15 different children tends to result in generalised care that is not closely attuned to any one child. It is also very difficult for any one of these various members of staff to have paid enough focused and consistent attention to a particular child to be in a position to give detailed and focused feedback to parents about their child's day.

A second aspect of the key person principle that is commonly misunderstood is that children will be restricted to relationships with their key person alone and forbidden or discouraged from interacting with other workers. This is to turn the key person principle on its head, with children having to fit in with this method of organisation rather than this method of organisation fitting in with what children need and want. The point of the key person principle is not to restrict children's interactions with other members of staff but to be sufficiently responsive when they want intimacy and closeness with 'their special member of staff'. When they do not want or need that, but prefer to interact with other staff members, then of course it would be wrong to restrict or try and prevent that in any way.

What do children say about the relationships they need?

Relationship is key: a child's perspective

In Meera Syal's novel *Anita and Me* (1997), the author describes a baby boy, Sunil, separating from his mother as he goes to nursery. By contrast, Angelina, a 2½-year-old toddler who was an object of another study (Elfer and Selleck 1999) attends a nursery where a key person approach has been developed.

We do not know how these children might have reacted in the early childhood institution described by Dahlberg *et al.* (1999). Nevertheless, we think the evidence from the children about separation is compelling.

Sunil's story

Sunil would be sleeping on her chest, a snuffling milky mass of warm roundness barring the way to her heart. He had to be forcibly peeled off her at nursery every morning, and stopped crying only when one of the carers sang mama's lullaby to him (mama had written it down in phonetic Hindi and adapted it to the tune of 'Baa Baa Black Sheep'). If she tried to put him down, he would clamp toes and fingers to any available expanse of flesh or material and if she left the room, he would cry, not the petulant, demanding cry of the child deprived of a toy, but great gulping sobs of abandonment and terror which would bring us all rushing to his side...But once in her arms, he would become the Sunil the rest of the world saw and loved, a smiling, dimpled, chubby, bite-sized morsel of cuteness, dispensing infant largesse from his throne, my mama.

(Syal 1997: 170)

Such a quotation is likely to provoke strongly diverse reactions in different readers as illustrated in Figure 1.1.

Why have we included this fictional extract? To bring to life the importance of having a key person in the nursery. Sunil's story shows the reality and depth of feelings that a very young child may have as part of his or her whole experience of nursery. But that does not mean that a baby or young child can only be settled and secure with a close family member.

Angelina's story

As part of a study of children in full-time nursery, Elfer and Selleck (1999) thought it would be interesting to examine Angelina to see what she could 'tell' us of her experience at nursery. Her behaviour is described in the following extract and various reactions to it can be seen in Figure 1.2.

> ...they are talking with each other. Joan's gestures and Angelina's responses suggest that they are talking about the leaves blowing off the trees at the end of the garden. Angelina is running and excitedly watching the leaves spin down from the tree to the ground as the wind blows them off the branches. Joan has at last found an activity which matches Angelina's need for action and engages her interest. Joan offers her sustained and individual attention. Angelina seems to be having a very enjoyable, animated and exciting time catching the spinning leaves one by one. After catching each leaf, she runs back to Joan to be lifted up with her, and to look again over the wall.
>
> Joan picks up Angelina when she comes to her and holds her lovingly and they watch the other children together. Angelina seems calmer and snuggles into her and watches the children over the other side of the wall sleepily. She seems to be more relaxed than I have ever seen her before.

(Elfer and Selleck 1999)

What are Sunil and Angelina telling us?

The different reactions show how Sunil's and Angelina's voices have been heard. Our responses to babies and young children's powerful communications, for example the baby crying in the supermarket or the toddler rigidly refusing to be strapped into his buggy, are likely to be full of mixed thoughts and feelings. How we react seems to depend not so much on our own internal states of stress or calmness, as on the external circumstances.

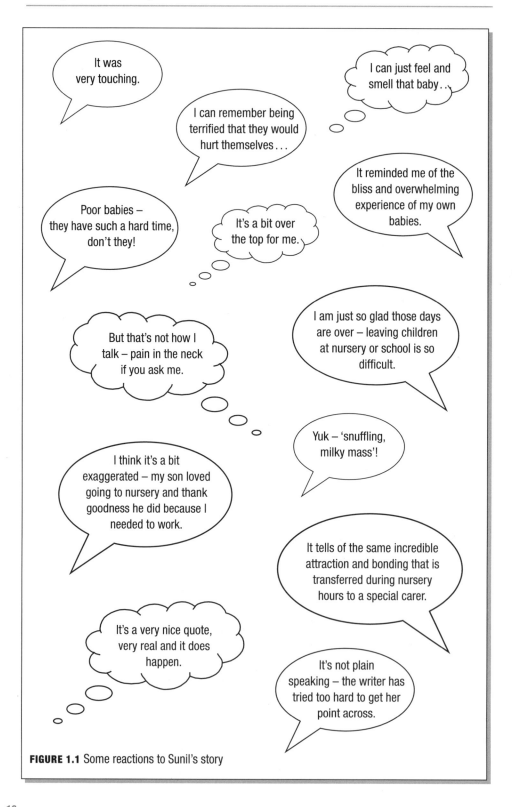

FIGURE 1.1 Some reactions to Sunil's story

FIGURE 1.2 Some reactions to Angelina's story

But if we put to one side these personal responses and focus instead on what Sunil and Angelina are telling us, two major messages emerge loud and clear:

- How much particular adults matter to them.
- What a huge difference these adults make to their emotional well-being and their ability to enjoy and learn from the opportunities around them.

2

What is the key person approach?

THE KEY PERSON APPROACH is a way of working in nurseries in which the whole focus and organisation is aimed at enabling and supporting close attachments between individual children and individual nursery staff. The key person approach is an involvement, an individual and reciprocal commitment between a member of staff and a family. It is an approach that has clear benefits for all involved.

The benefits of a key person approach

For babies and young children: The key person(s) makes sure that, within the day-to-day demands of a nursery each child feels special and individual, cherished and thought about by someone in particular while they are away from home. It is as though the child were 'camped out in the key person's mind' or that there is an elastic thread of attachment that allows for being apart as well as for being together. The child in the nursery will experience a close relationship that is affectionate and reliable.

For parents, particularly mothers: The key person(s) approach ensures that parents have the opportunity to build a personal relationship with 'someone' rather than 'all of them' working in the nursery. The benefits are likely to be peace of mind and the possibility of building a partnership with professional staff who may share with them the pleasures and stresses of child-rearing. It gives parents the chance to liaise with someone else who is fully committed and familiar with their baby or child.

For the key person: The key person approach is intense, hard work and a big commitment. This relationship makes very real physical, intellectual and emotional demands upon the key person and these need to be understood, planned for and supported by the nursery policies and management. One of the benefits of being and becoming a key person is the sense that you really matter to a child and to their family. You are likely to have a powerful impact on the child's well-being, their mental health, and their chances to think and learn. These powers and responsibilities will engender feelings of pleasure and pain, the joy and relief of partings and reunions, and the satisfaction and anxiety of being a key person in a child's formative early years care and education.

For the nursery: The key person approach leads to better-satisfied and engaged staff, improved care and learning for the children, and a parent clientele who are likely to develop a more trusting confidence in the competencies, qualities and devotion of professional staff. There are indications that this approach reduces staff sickness and absence, and develops involvement and positive attitudes to professional development within staff teams.

Why 'key person' and not 'key worker'?

The terms 'key worker' and 'key person' are often used interchangeably in nurseries as well as in other areas of social care, for example in hospitals or in work with people with mental or physical disabilities. We would like to draw a clear distinction between the two terms. A 'key worker' is often used to describe a role in which the focus is on liaison or coordinating between different professionals or disciplines, making sure that services work in a coordinated way. It is quite different from the 'key person' role defined above. The term 'key worker' is also used to describe how staff work strategically in nurseries to enhance smooth organisation and record-keeping. This is only one part of being a key person, which is an emotional relationship as well as an organisational strategy.

The key person approach for babies and young children

The first few years, and especially the first 12 months, are a very sensitive, special, exciting, anxious, often overwhelming time for a young child. If nurseries work well, they may be able to provide a deeply satisfying and enriching experience for the youngster. This is *not replacing* but *supplementing* the loving care and learning time children need at home.

As babies move towards crawling, toddling and more confident walking, they are also able to seek out the adults they need. The availability of one main adult whom they can count on is very important to them. That person can provide the baby with a sense of being special, even of being loved, secure and thought about.

During our work in a wide range of nurseries, parents often tell us that while they want their child to make special relationships with adults in the nursery, they would rather these didn't be come 'too special'. However close the relationships a child might make in nursery, relationships at home are usually the most constant, this being the safest and soundest place from which children may move on to other friendships and connections with many affectionate and interesting people. The key close people in the nursery might have to change from time to time, so it is important that parents remain the most stable and strong starting place from which to venture out.

Of course, the key person cannot be there every minute of the day; no one, even at home, can manage, or would even aspire to manage, that. Otherwise, how would children ever learn that they could survive if left alone for a short time? How would they realise that the people who love them or who are concerned for them will not forget them but will come back as soon as possible?

Some babies and children are in the nursery from around eight in the morning until six in the evening – ten hours. Very few staff work shifts that long and obviously the key person will go on holiday, be off sick, or will have to attend to something else during a child's time at nursery. *It is at these times that a back-up key person is so important.* Even so, the periods when the main key person is not available must be kept to a minimum or the role starts to become meaningless.

The key person is the staff member who has begun to get to know the important adults and brothers and sisters at home, who knows the baby or young child well, and is aware of all the special details of how he or she is cared for. This can be done in different ways. Sometimes home visits are possible. For some nurseries this may be difficult, but it might be possible to arrange special times when the parent(s) can come to the nursery rather than trying to talk at the beginning or end of the day, which are usually such busy times. In some cases a long phone call can be scheduled. Sometimes this communication will have to be done partly in writing with home/nursery diary exchanges. The key person is the staff member who has planned with the family when the baby will start at nursery; how they will work together to introduce the child and settle him or her in; how they will combine efforts to make sure life in the nursery and life at home dovetails together.

Nursery and home are not the same thing and the key person approach is not about trying to make them so. In nursery, the baby or young child has opportunities for experiences that he or she could not have at home.

However, home and nursery do need to 'fit together' well, and that calls for regular dialogue between parents and the key person, who together must become partners, giving the baby or young child a sense of reassurance that they can come to reach agreements about his or her daily care. This will also reduce the demands on the baby or child to adapt to lots of different adults or ways of being handled.

The key person is the staff member who is there, *as far as possible*, to greet the baby or child in the morning, to provide comfort if the youngster is upset, to play and enjoy time with him or her, and to be the one, whenever possible, to offer intimate bodily care. This staff member will also have other children for whom she is a key person and part of the skill of her job is being available to each of these children, in turn and sometimes together, as much as she can. Of course, the demands of nursery organisation and the fact that she has only one pair of hands means she cannot do everything for everybody all of the time.

What is certain is that children who are enabled to feel safe and secure will be much more able to be themselves and to try out new ideas in the various relationships and experiences on offer in the nursery.

The complexity and power of the key person approach from the point of view of babies and young children is illustrated vividly in the following two cases studies. In the first, researcher Carmen Dalli (2000) describes the finer details of 16-month-old Nina settling into nursery and the possible meanings of Nina's behaviour as she separates from her mother and encounters the new world of nursery.

Case Study **Nina is settled into nursery**

09.40   'So I'll just say goodbye to her,' says mum to Sarah – she bends towards Nina across the dough table and says, 'Nina, sweetie, goodbye, bye Nina.' Nina is very absorbed in dough play, however, and does not really look up. 'Bye, bye, ta ta,' says mum again. But there's still no response from Nina. Mum says, 'I sort of feel I should get some recognition from her that I'm going,' and tries again. Mum waves and waves, but there still is no acknowledgement by Nina. Mum tries again with no response, so mum leaves without Nina having realised this. Sarah and Nina play at rolling the dough and pretending to eat little balls of it.

For the next few minutes, Nina remained quite happily occupied in dough play with Sarah, sometimes watching with interest, with her left hand on Sarah's knee, as Sarah made some dough 'snakes' and at other times rolling out dough herself. When one of the dough 'snakes' fell onto the floor, Nina happily complied with Sarah's request to pick it up. Nina gave the first sign that she might be aware of her mother's absence about 10 minutes

---

after Jean's departure when she looked up from the table and looked around the room searchingly. This behaviour led Sarah to comment quietly to me, 'Did you see her searching?' As Nina's attention was caught by a doll's pushchair, however, the moment passed, and it was not till three minutes later that Nina suddenly again appeared to become aware that her mother was absent. This 'realisation' was recorded in this way:

> 09.52   Nina walks off towards the hallway, a paintbrush in her hand and back again to the easel – Sarah takes the paintbrush off her, picking up an apron and saying, 'Oh, Nina,' looking at her paint-covered hands. Nina turns away and walks off again towards the hallway and on towards the front door.

> 09.53   Nina starts to cry at the front door and looks 'lost' as if she has just realised that mum is not around. Sarah follows her in the hallway; she picks Nina up and takes her to the bathroom to wash the paint off her hands. Sarah talks about the handwashing and the paint coming off as they do this. When they finish, Nina has stopped crying, and Sarah puts her down on the floor; but Nina walks back to the centre front door and cries again.

> 09.54   Sarah follows; she picks Nina up and gives her a kiss. Nina stops crying – they walk to the blue-carpeted room where an older boy is playing with a toy dog. Sarah talks to the boy and asks if Nina can look at his toy dog – Nina smiles broadly at this and is now distracted by the dog and then the flexi-tunnel and then the Lego firehouse that Sarah starts to play with.

While it is not possible to be sure what Nina's 'real' intentions were in going to the centre's front door during these incidents, it is difficult to escape the interpretation that Nina had realised that her mother had left the centre and that she possibly wished to follow her. Sarah had a similar interpretation – both in her comment about Nina's 'searching' behaviour and her immediate actions to distract Nina while washing her hands, and in her actions to comfort and distract her again with the affectionate kiss and playing in the blue room.

What was also interesting in the interaction between Nina and Sarah during the first trial-separation session was the change in the behaviour between Sarah and Nina when Jean was not present. As I noted above, Sarah had been involved in a variety of interactions with Nina while Jean had been present; however, true to her principle that 'when mum is here, I'm not the primary caregiver', Sarah had kept largely in the background and had allowed Nina to explore the centre alongside her mother. During this session, however, from the time of Jean's departure to her return, Sarah was constantly at Nina's side. This proximity did not appear to perturb Nina, who seemed to easily accept comfort from Sarah and to let her 'take her (Nina's) mind off mum not being there'. There were no further obvious signs that Nina was conscious of her mother's absence during the first trial-separation session, although the reunion with Jean was, from an observer's point of view, an emotional one, with Jean's face looking flushed with pleasure and Nina's face beaming with delight. Sarah's account to Jean of Nina's response to the separation was factual in detail and included the evaluation that Nina had been 'excellent'. Jean looked at me for verification, and I smiled and nodded, wondering, not for the last time, about how much I should become involved in these interactions.

In the next case study, Dorothy Selleck (2001: 87), in a support and professional development role to the staff of a nursery, notes how the staff tune and adapt the possibilities for learning in response to children's own ideas and initiatives.

Case Study | A curriculum 'fit' for babies and toddlers

There has been more emphasis on the 'preparation of the room', than on observing the learning of children in it. This has sometimes resulted in a mismatch of curriculum for babies and toddlers. Observation of what children are really interested in, an emphasis on the **received** curriculum (through observation) rather than the planned curriculum (based on developmental stages) does seem to make a difference to children's enjoyment and involvement in their play.

For instance Ibrahim left his repetitive pushchair-pacing round the garden when Joan observed his interest in a patch of soil. She fetched a selection of spades so that he could 'dig for worms'. Ibrahim initiated this new, but unplanned garden activity.

Oumou chose to press the buttons of the photocopier as Sita copied letters to the parents, rather than to play in the activity set up for the group. Oumou chose to be alongside Sita. If Joan and Sita had stuck with the planned curriculum, rather than be influenced by the toddlers' preoccupations, the quality of the child's play and learning is likely to have been 'lower level' (DfEE 2000).

Watching, and listening to a child makes a difference. Each child is likely to be more involved in meaningful activities for them when the curriculum is matched to their interests and they are engaged in shared purpose with others. Ibrahim didn't find a worm but pocketed his own buried coin, Oumou was delighted with the clean printed sheets she produced for Sita!

The key person approach for parents, particularly mothers

It was wonderful to leave him with someone we trusted completely. We knew she understood the real William. She gave him the time and the right encouragement to develop his confidence and become the chatterbox that he is at home.

(Glover and Glover 2001; personal communication with authors)

The decision to relinquish part of the care and teaching of your baby or child to the staff in a nursery is a big step. This leaves some parents feeling anxious and uncertain. Ideally parents would be in a position to help their baby or child settle into the nursery with great sensitivity and empathy, but if parents have not had sufficient opportunity to get to know and trust the nursery staff, then their anxiety and uncertainty about leaving their child in a setting with which they are not sufficiently confident may make it doubly difficult to help their child manage the separation in the best possible way. Babies and young children, fearful or anxious about whether this new situation will be safe enough for them, will certainly pick up on their parents' similarly fearful or anxious feelings.

The parents may find it hard to leave or, when they have left, feel very distracted and worried. Sometimes the anxiety and uncertainty seem to have the opposite effect and parents might appear almost too casual to nursery staff, perhaps even a bit uncaring, as they want to flee the pain of being upset or seeing their child's distress by hurrying through any settling-in time. At other times, parents may feel nothing but delight and relief when their child joins in with their nursery play almost without a backward glance. However, this very same scenario may just as easily evoke feelings of abandonment, jealousy, and secret resentment at the ease with which their child is embraced by the nursery and leaves their home attachments.

These different ways of feeling and behaving are means of coping with the act of parting and with any feelings of guilt, anxiety and resentment that may go with it. The key person approach is to help manage these feelings. The key person can help to make the parting a dignified and carefully thought-out time, even if it is quite a brief affair, rather than a hurried, embarrassed handing over and rushing away. This will enable the mother or father to feel reasonably confident that they have made the right decision in placing their baby or child in a particular nursery. It will reassure them that their child will be well looked after by mainly one person who will help them to keep in touch with their child.

Beyond this important time of settling in, it is vital that parents have an opportunity to build a close relationship with their child's key person as this provides a means through which their concerns may be taken into account by the nursery. Some parents, while valuing what the nursery gives to their child, also speak of a slight sense of missing out on what their child does each day. Part of the key person relationship for parents is knowing that 'someone', rather than 'all of them' are particularly looking forward to seeing them and talking with them as they hand over or reunite with their child. It is knowing that there is a personal service that will enable their child to go gently from 'one lap' at home to another at nursery.

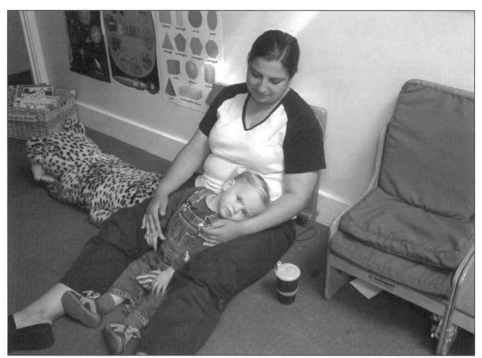

A child being settled into the nursery. After separating from his parents the key person stays physically close and available to the child. The child has time to take in the surroundings and time to choose where to play next, as he is held safely in the comforting, containing lap of his key person. His special toy and drinking cup are close by to sustain connections with home, and the key person observes and holds him attentively as he looks inquiringly, warily, at the other activities and people in the nursery.

This is where parents' personal stories of their bad night or the thrill of seeing their child's first experiences (of a waterfall, a new rhyme learnt, or their preoccupation with emptying the wastepaper bin), may be shared with humour, with empathy, or in seriousness, and in shared affection for the child. In response the child's key person uses this time to pass the parent a snapshot of their child's day. Not only the efficient information of meals eaten and things played with (an important part of customer client services), but more importantly, a personal story from someone they trust to tell them the things they really want to know about. Parents in a key person relationship will be able to be in a conversation with that special person. This kind of conversation with a parent can even be worth staying late for as the key person will hear some of the details rather than the 'developmental report'. It can be infinitely more satisfying than the parent urgently communicating the essentials to 'the staff' as their employer/customer in the nursery service.

A child and her key person enjoying play together in the outside learning area. This is a special person to share her excitement with as she makes new discoveries and learns new skills. Later she may go on to play with other children and other adults as she gains confidence in her play with the new tyre game.

The key person approach for the key person

In a recent questionnaire, staff were asked about their feelings about working in the centre. Almost all staff expressed a high level of satisfaction in their work, and commitment to children and families in their key person groups, and to their own continuing professional development. The ability to plan and care for their own group of children motivated staff who frequently described themselves as 'happy' in their work.

(Duffy 2000)

For members of staff, the key person approach can make their job much more satisfying. There is evidence of fewer absences, and staff are less likely to move on when they experience the particular responsibilities and pleasures of being involved with a few children in particular. We also know that this special relationship between child and key person in the nursery does not compromise the close bonds between parents and children at home (National Institute of Child Health and Human Development Early Child Care Research Network 1997). The parents will always be the most significant people in a child's life and personal interactions between staff and parents – where trust, as well as anxieties (mistrust), can be spoken about – can be professionally challenging and worthwhile.

Looking after someone else's baby on a day-to-day basis in a nursery is a complex job involving a great deal of responsibility and trust on all sides. We believe that it only really works well for the staff when this is recognised, talked about, and supported. There is all too often little recognition of the sustained physical, emotional and intellectual demands made on the key person. The physical demands of the day are considerable and can be reduced by reviewing how lifting and carrying is undertaken and whether it is being done unnecessarily.

The emotional demands are great too. The key person is in a professional role but she must develop a very personal and intimate relationship with each of the babies and children with whom she is working. There are bound to be some painful feelings involved, as the work cannot be done in an emotionally anaesthetised way. Building individual relationships with children before help-ing them to move on when it is time to leave, and always being mindful that the parents are the most important adults in their lives, are just two aspects of the job that are bound to touch some of a key person's own personal experiences of close relationships, beginnings and endings. Sometimes staff speak of 'loving a child to bits', then in the next breath talk of all the children in only a general and vague way. Maintaining an appropriate professional intimacy, which every child needs in order to feel special, while keeping an appropriate professional distance, requires emotional work of the highest calibre.

The key person approach for the nursery

The key person approach provides a focus for the organisation of the nursery. Experience of existing systems suggests that staff are more satisfied and engaged. When staff have an attachment to particular children – rather than a merely affectionate interest in all the children in their room group – they are less likely to need time off from the stresses of managing many children at once. Fewer staff absences and lower staff turnover mean benefits all round for nurseries; there is more opportunity for continuity in developing good-quality policies and practices, and greater retention of more experienced staff (Raikes 1996; Hay 1996).

Professional intimacy and stability in the relationships between adults assigned to small groups of particular children are also likely to provide better care and learning experiences matched to children's cultural and devel-opmental needs (Munn and Schaffer 1993; Hopkins 1988).

Parents are likely to develop greater confidence in the competencies, qualities and commitment of the nursery as a service. When families are involved with a particular nursery worker, who is systematically supported and managed by more-experienced and highly trained professional managers, the professional status and standing of a nursery in the community is likely to be enhanced (Raikes 1996).

3

A strategy for implementation

IN THIS CHAPTER WE describe the three dimensions (illustrated in Figure 3.1) which, during our work with nursery managers and practitioners, have emerged as the nuts and bolts of how to implement the key person approach.

Building anything, including effective practice in nursery work, depends on good foundations. The starting point of the key person approach needs to be based on a firm grasp of the values, principles and research evidence presented in Chapter 2. Practical experience has shown that such a way of working, while paying dividends, does not make for an easy life in terms of the organisational and emotional demands that are raised.

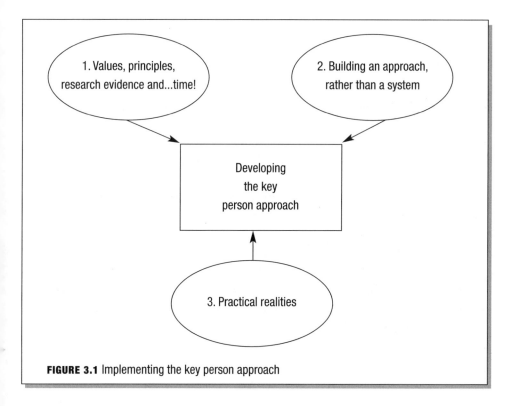

FIGURE 3.1 Implementing the key person approach

Values, principles, research evidence and . . . time!

Each setting should set aside time to read and think about the research evidence presented in Chapter 2: how does it fit with their own experience, values and principles? One of the hardest aspects is simply when to find the time for staff to sit down and consider the evidence together as a team.

In the wide range of nursery settings, from small private nurseries to large centres of excellence, time is extremely limited. Very few nurseries have regular or scheduled meeting time, and maintaining the 1 : 3 ratio that national standards require for the youngest children is a continual challenge. Staying behind at the end of a shift for a team meeting is exhausting. Building in professional development time for all practitioners, as part of the working week rather than in addition to it, must be a priority, as well as one of the standards by which we compare our national system of provision with that of other countries.

In the absence of that right to specific professional development time as part of the working week, as yet, nurseries are managing to create thinking space for groups of staff to respond to research evidence and to reflect on its relevance in a particular setting. From time to time, managers release a member of staff to join a working group with representatives from other nurseries; alternatively, it is done at the end of shifts in staff's own time. Sometimes, in larger 'extended day' nurseries, there may be periods of time during the day or week when there are fewer children in the setting, at which point a small group of staff can meet together.

There are also examples where this process of linking research and practice has been facilitated by bringing in specialist consultants to lead professional development sessions for managers and practitioners to update their knowledge and understanding of the key person approach. Solid and up-to-date knowledge of the rationale of the approach – and dissenting views – will inform managers' planning, before they begin working with their staff teams.

The 'statement of commitment' shown in Figure 3.2 comes from a London nursery's handbook. Research evidence is crucial, but research papers are not normally accessible and easily absorbed so that staff can turn them into practice the next day! The research evidence needs to be digested and turned into a 'working statement' that can be understood by parents and staff as a statement of 'our approach':

What is a key person?

What is a key person? The key person is the special member of staff who comes to visit you and your child at home (if you would like a home visit), who gets to know you and your child, and who welcomes you and your child to the nursery. The key person will never ever replace the parent, but will be a special extra adult for your child. We believe that this essential attachment should be planned for and encouraged. As your child gains confidence, then she or he will move happily away from the key person and start to get to know the other staff in the nursery. But the key person is still there, for you and your child, as a special person who gets to know you and who is there whenever she or he is needed.

FIGURE 3.2 Statement of commitment (from Woodlands Park Nursery Centre's *Information for Parents*)

Building an approach, rather than a system

We have referred to the key person as an 'approach' rather than a system; this is particularly important in making the key person a reality in nurseries. It is so much about human relationships but, more than this, it is about very young children's relationships with adults. The voices, wishes and feelings of children seem often not to be heard or valued, and the younger the child, the more this seems to be the case.

Seeing and hearing through each child's eyes and ears, putting ourselves in their shoes, and responding to their need for intimacy and attachment while not imposing it, all seem to be understood in nurseries as a way of working – an approach that needs developing and perfecting over time. It cannot really be addressed simply as a system of organisation that can be implemented by putting a rota on the wall.

Getting the right kind of key person approach underway needs some definite action by managers, supervisors, experienced staff and newly appointed carers. But change is difficult: it needs to be motivated and driven by a spirit of advocacy for the rights of children to be listened to, even before they can speak. This is no 'pie in the sky' outcome:

> The Mosaic approach has been developed with three and four year olds in an early childhood institution and has been adapted to work with children under two, children for whom English is an additional language, keyworkers and parents...The phrase 'voice of the child' may suggest the transmission of ideas only through words, but listening to young children, including pre-verbal children, needs to be a

process which is open to the many creative ways young children can use to express their views and experiences. Malaguzzi's phrase 'the hundred languages of children' reminds us of this potential.

(Clark and Moss 2001: 1)

People will give many 'good reasons' why the key person approach cannot be developed. Some may say it is not possible. Others may not even believe it is really desirable. Still others may say that there is no need to do anything because 'we have such an approach already'. Sometimes the objections seem to be based on a view of the key person approach as unrealistic:

'You can't have a key person approach because there is no way you can be there all the time for your key children – you may not be on duty when they arrive in the morning or you may be off duty before they go home.'

(Elfer, forthcoming)

Well yes! Any approach that seeks to ensure the same person is there ALL the time is bound to fail. But as we said earlier, not even a parent can do this for their child and it is through brief and longer separations, although painful, that children learn they can be separated and manage for a short time independently of the people they love.

Sometimes the objections seem almost absurd:

'You can't have a key person approach because you have got to work as a team. Otherwise you would have a situation where a child is about to have an accident or something and the member of staff seeing it says, "Oh I can't do anything because it is not my key child."'

(Ibid.)

We think such concerns can be better understood as a member of staff expressing wider anxieties about the consequences of the key person approach. She may really be afraid that making individual relationships will lead to a lack of fairness in the way children are treated or even that some children may come to be neglected whilst others receive 'too much' attention.

Juliet Hopkins (1988: 103) has shown the depth of some staff anxieties:

Nursery nurses believed that children should be treated equally and given equal attention, or else some would miss out. In practice, this seemed to mean avoiding any lengthy involvements with individual children, for fear that others were being ignored or getting jealous; they also feared that favoured children might become spoiled. The nursery nurses' struggle not to favour some children more than others emerged in the discussions as a reaction against the strong wish to do so. Their feelings towards the children were not at all equal; they found some of them appealing and loveable, others uninteresting, some annoying and a few unbearable. The nursery nurses deprecated their biases and felt especially guilty about their dislike of some of the children. It was a relief to them to discover that the group leaders regarded this as a problem to be understood rather than as a failure to be condemned.

However, these feelings emerged only over an extended period of meetings. We think the last sentence is crucial to developing the key person approach in nurseries. Managers have a vital role, not just in their ingenuity for creating time for talking, but in creating a climate of attitudes that sees talking about heartfelt worries or concerns as a positive part of the developing professional life of the nursery rather than being 'difficult' or 'awkward'.

Failure to take account of these underlying anxieties explains why some nurseries' key person approaches do not seem to translate into practice: 'We have often seen in nurseries a child's supposed key person attending to impersonal tasks whilst he was fed or comforted by another staff member' (Goldschmied and Jackson 1994: 38). As Vernon and Smith (1994: 81) witnessed during one of their studies:

> Five of the fifteen nurseries visited were amongst those who . . . stated that they did not make use of a keyworker arrangement . . . however, having said this, the effects of the arrangements such nurseries did have in place did not always appear to be markedly different from those achieved by nurseries which stated that they did operate a keyworker system.

The nursery manager or owner will not have all the answers – she faces some difficult challenges. Part of the key person approach is the process of working and struggling together to:

- hear everyone's point of view
- help each other develop ideas and possibilities
- put proposals into practice and try them out
- build on what seems to work and to find another way when something does not.

But this must be maintained as a shared responsibility. Nursery practitioners rightly expect to be consulted about and involved in decisions regarding professional practices. But one manager told us that, having done this, some staff responded by saying 'well you're the manager, you decide'.

But being the one 'to decide' is not realistic. All the managers we have spoken to about the key person approach said that there was not a blueprint. The process of implementation depended not on any 'right decision' but rather on a continual determination to keep the key person approach on the agenda. In practice, this involved continually moving back and forth between principles, evidence and statements of commitment on the one hand, and solving practical questions, within each nursery's particular circumstances, on the other.

Practical realities

Home visits and establishing a partnership

The staff of Woodlands Park Nursery Centre make it clear in their *Information for Parents* (see Figure 3.2) that the home visit is the starting point for their key person approach. But they are sensitive to it being the parents' right to decide whether they want such a visit. As the starting point of a partnership between home and nursery in the care of a child, this consciousness of the dynamics of power – 'who is in charge and how are things decided', the importance of decisions being shared and being seen to be shared – seems essential in setting the pattern of how decisions will be collectively made and information exchanged as the child's career in nursery continues.

A key person in the nursery sharing a book with a child. Both of them are facing the pages together and sharing the experiences that they have together been a part of, or that have been related by the child's parents. The adult makes connections with the past experiences so that the child can make sense of new ones.

In private nurseries, this relationship can seem quite different to that experienced with a local authority centre. Having a 'customer orientation' is good business practice in any enterprise. When the business is a nursery and the customer is the parent, the power relationship between parent and nursery is likely to shift from 'Will this nursery want to give my child a place?' to 'Will this parent want to buy a place in my nursery?' Understandably, in the latter case, nursery staff may be afraid to talk about home visits or a settling-in process in case these are seen by the parents as unnecessary or inconvenient and lead to the parent going elsewhere. The reality of a shortage of places may make this unlikely. The staff of private nurseries, however, need the clear support of managers and owners to negotiate and plan a partnership between nursery and home where the child remains clearly in focus as a 'customer' too.

The benefits, and potential for partnership, of the home visit seem more than evident in the following parent's description of her child starting at a nursery in the London Borough of Camden:

'When we had our home visit I explained how Liam loves pottering round the flat trailing anything with a flex behind him, like the vacuum cleaner or my hair dryer. On his first day Leon [the nursery worker] had put out lengths of string tied to little toys and, in the garden, there were lengths of garden hose. I was amazed, and touched, at the care and interest he'd taken.'

(Manning Morton and Thorpe 2001: section 8, p. 3)

Building a key group

This has been one of the most difficult parts of the book to write. Should the linking of new children to the nursery with a particular key person, and building the key group of children for whom a key person is responsible, be largely a matter of 'who clicks with who' or should it be a more definitely managed and directed activity?

Sometimes children or parents make spontaneous links with a particular member of staff in nursery (perhaps the member of staff who showed them around when they first visited the setting). It may then seem 'natural' that this member of staff should become the key person for that child and his or her family. There may be scope to take into account such 'linking' in allocating children to a particular key person.

We would argue, however, that to be allow this to be the main allocation system in the nursery would undermine the need for the key person approach to be integrated into the nursery's overall management arrangements.

First, the role of key person needs to be a proactive one. A central part of the role of being a key person is to get to know a family, ask parents and carers to share information about home life and background and to learn about the religious, linguistic and cultural background of the family. Secondly, spontaneous links will happen in a few cases, but the parents or carers of most of the new babies and young children entering nursery will not know a member of staff or have had any basis for expressing a preference.

We are concerned that the idea of links forming in a natural or spontaneous way – or of families gravitating towards particular members of staff, or vice versa – may suggest a misleadingly simple process. We think it denies, or certainly underplays, the central management function of balancing the overall intake of children to nursery and positive, managed allocation. By this we mean ensuring each child is allocated to a key person, taking active account of the size of that key person's existing group of children and of that person's availability to settle a new child (for example, have they just embarked on settling another child? Are they about to go on holiday?).

Sensitivity to each family's home language and culture is a central objective of the key person approach. Yet, the very concept of a 'key person' may be unfamiliar in some cultures. A Chinese parent, while receptive to the provision of a special relationship in nursery between a key person and her child, could not relate this to her own experience of childcare relationships in her part of China. In the English nursery her child attended, the key person was able to find out about the different values and priorities of nursery provision in China and be more sensitive to this parent's background and expectations.

In the following three examples, we focus on particular aspects of developing the key person approach, in different kinds of nurseries. The first example is taken from a group of private nurseries while the second and third examples are from individual nurseries. These are three examples of nurseries in very different circumstances and at different stages in the development and sophistication of their approach.

The examples demonstrate the plurality of the practical task of *making it work* alongside the *group work* processes of finding innovative ways of translating the staff groups' principles into practice. In each of these nurseries the process of developing the key person approach begins with a commitment to the necessity, the cruciality, of ensuring that all the children and their families had an entitlement to a special attachment relationship with one member of staff – a designated person to support the mental health, well-being, care and learning of each child enrolled in their nursery. Each nursery had different starting points and is developing its approach in different ways. The pace of development is being dictated by the staff processes of finding new ways of working together which most people can agree to.

Example 1: The nursery group

A group of private nurseries with branches across England decided to establish a key person approach in each nursery.

The nursery group created the key national post of Director of Quality and Training in direct response to Ofsted's 2001 requirements for inspections to ensure national-quality standards; as well as embracing the company's aspirations to provide customers with the best possible service. Most customers are working parents requiring full-time day care for babies through to five-year-olds.

The company appointed an experienced nursery manager with a recent Master's degree in Early Childhood Studies. Her brief was to develop a high-quality service through a coordinated, professional-development training programme.

She identified her priorities by:

■ carrying out an audit of the training needs of *all* nursery staff, as identified by them and their managers;

■ identifying the theoretical underpinnings for the design of the Quality Programme, based on her recent study and review of the latest research, as well as taking account of the company's existing ethos;

■ sending all parents a questionnaire: what were their expectations of quality in the nursery?

The Director of Quality and Training was able to identify key responses from which the company's key person approach was developed. Her findings revealed that parents:

■ wanted continuity of care for their babies with as few changes in personnel as possible;

■ valued the connection with 'one of them' rather than 'everyone' when handing over their little children;

■ wanted a person they could contact by phone and text message, as well as the person-to-person contacts at the beginning and end of the day;

■ needed a reliable, dependable and flexible service so they were 'free' to concentrate on work;

■ wanted to know there was someone there who 'loved their babies too, and who *really* listened to what they wanted for their children'.

These responses – which reflected the Director's personal and professional convictions – provided the motivation and commitment to implement a key person approach. They were seen as being at the heart of developing a high-quality and distinctive nursery practice. Her personal charisma and professional authority have been central to the company developing a key person approach.

Next, she designed a staged programme for the implementation of this new approach:

1 A series of meetings with the sales and marketing team was arranged to develop a strategic approach to promote a quality service attuned for children and parents through the key person approach. Establishing the key person approach as a *selling point* should *underpin* the quality of the service. They agreed to redesign their printed marketing material to incorporate an explanation of the key person approach, citing the benefits for parents and children, as well as the commitments needed for parents to plan for an extended settling-in period. This was judged important if the nursery was to remain competitive. It was also agreed that staff handling initial enquiries from prospective customers would have some basic training in explaining this new approach.

2 A series of training programmes for nursery managers was designed to induct them into the theoretical underpinning of a key person approach; to discuss the implications for the deployment of personnel and resources; admissions of children; and the design of a staff-training programme.

3 The company decided to introduce the new approach gradually, after staff had been trained and were ideologically and technically prepared for this new way of working. The management team worked hard to consider the implications of these changes. They endeavoured to predict issues to be addressed at each stage without wavering from their resolution to overcome the practical difficulties in the best interests of the children. For example, they anticipated pressures from within nurseries, to accelerate the settling-in time. The sales and marketing staff – as well as the nursery staff – anticipated pressures from parents to 'hurry through' a settling-in process that was seen to be essential in a key person approach. Understandably, everyone wanted to make the nursery seem as easy and flexible to use as possible for potential parent customers. Establishing how available and flexible parents can be during their child's settling-in period might seem like being a 'nuisance' and an unnecessary complication for a parent trying to meet work commitments. This needed to be addressed in training at all levels.

As we write, this story of development continues. The company has not yet addressed the issues of practical arrangements for admissions, or how to organise key person nursery groups. But we must emphasise the care and attention to detail the company took in laying the groundwork for making the key person approach effective. They achieved this, in particular, by:

- seeking the views of parents on their expectations of nursery;
- enabling the development of a clear theoretical underpinning to the key person approach;
- explaining the benefits of the approach for parents and children, and being realistic about its demands;
- anticipating the pressure to 'hurry through' the settling-in period.

In the second nursery, the development of the key person approach is more advanced.

Example 2: The new Nursery Centre

The key person approach in this nursery began with reorganisation: staff from a social services nursery joined with staff from a nursery school to form a new Nursery Centre.

This new staff team has had a number of team-building sessions as part of a planned process to unite the two different culture groups of care and education. Management decided that all staff would work in cycles with the whole age range of children (18 months to five years old). This represented a significant change, and was met with cautious optimism by some and resistance by others! However, a policy was developed based on the belief that continuity of curriculum as well as constancy in personnel was the bedrock for meeting the needs of children. Many children and families had experienced difficult transitions and family crises. The nursery accommodates a wide range of family needs including those of asylum seekers, refugees and families in turmoil with health or social pressures, as well as those of families where both parents choose or need to work. The staff identified a key person approach as important for children and families, as well as a way of enhancing a 'joined-up' working ethos and practice for the two staff groups becoming one.

In this centre, children are allocated a key person who settles them when they begin at 18 months, and then continues with them as they move through to the nursery centre for children aged 3 and over. The key person will then stay with the children and support them with their transition into a primary school. This innovative work offers an example of the organisational challenge as well as commitment to the theory and practice of this way of working.

The principles of the key person approach are maintained and the challenges met by a Development Team made up of the Senior Management

Team, representatives from the staff working directly with children, and an outside mentor/consultant. The team work together on practical issues from admissions through to curriculum, and meet regularly to review progress.

The discussion notes from one of these sessions, recorded in Figure 3.3, illustrate the range and detail of issues covered in these development group meetings and may offer foci for practical developments in other nurseries.

In the second nursery example, there are many detailed 'organisational challenges' for the Senior Management Team. These present an important contrast to the careful groundwork being carried out in the first nursery. We think the care taken to address these challenges is crucial to how well the key person approach is working out in practice. This example shows clearly how each nursery needs to solve its own organisational and practical issues of implementing and monitoring its key person approach if all staff are to be involved in, and committed to, 'making it work'. No set of guidelines can fit every nursery, but these two nurseries show different approaches and different stages of the development process. We also see how nursery teams are identifying and documenting the tasks they need to do next.

Example 3: The small, private nursery

As with the nursery in Example 2, it was an external event that created the opportunity, or rather the *need*, to develop the key person approach. Nursery three is privately owned, and offers full- and part-time places to 42 children aged between 4 months and five years old. The owner/manager established the nursery in her own home, offering places to 21 children. As a home-based nursery, it reflected the owner's personal ethos: small, intimate and homely, with each child and family well known to each member of staff. It also allowed these close relationships between staff and children to develop without the need for active organisation and systems to make this happen.

But an expanding nursery based in the home of a growing family is bound to lead to pressures on emotional as well as physical space. In February 2001, the nursery moved to premises that offered a separate physical space, as well as enough extra space to double the numbers of children. The owner/manager was presented with a tremendous sense of opportunity but also faced the risk that the closeness and intimacy of nursery relationships built up in a home environment, and developed over nearly a decade, would be lost.

The individual relationships that had arisen so spontaneously between staff, children and their families now seemed much less likely to develop unless specific plans were put into place.

Yet in contrast to the nursery group or the large Nursery Centre case studies, there is no realistic opportunity in a small private nursery to close for training or professional development days and there is certainly no Director of Quality and Training! The realities of managing a small business – ensuring financial viability and offering a reliable service to parents and secure employment to staff – places a high priority on continuity of service and maintenance of fee income. This nursery closed in the owner's home on a Friday and opened again in its new premises on the following Monday with no break of service to the children and families. Planning and thinking about closeness and continuity of relationships, therefore, had to be built in along-side an enormous variety of practical tasks.

However, the introduction of the National Day Care Standards (Ofsted 2001) – and growing encouragement for the private sector to strive for a culture of excellence by the adoption of quality assurance schemes such as the Investors in Children scheme proposed by DfES, or the National Day Nurseries Association Quality Counts scheme – means that creating space for such good practice should become more feasible.

In order to prepare the ground for this major change of size and site, but also with a determined commitment to ensuring children felt a sense of belonging and being special in the new nursery, the owner/manager began to plan for implementing a key person approach. She asked her staff to read about the 'key worker' approach as described by Goldschmied and Jackson (1994).

In retrospect, the owner/manager feels this was an important starting point but, as always, reading theory in a book is only the very first step in the journey of making it happen in practice. The staff members were asked to discuss the approach in a staff meeting. Finding time for staff meetings is a significant problem for small nursery businesses, which need to recover the cost of closing during working hours. Asking staff to stay on after work for staff meetings is not straightforward either.

But this nursery seems to have found an effective compromise between recognising the needs of the staff to have their evenings off, and the need for them to participate in regular professional development sessions. So it is built into contracts: all staff must attend an evening staff meeting about once every six weeks. The meeting is carefully structured with a clear agenda; discussion is professional and focused, and meetings last no longer than two hours. The staff are not paid but get a hot meal, making it a bit of a social occasion and a real model of the needs of staff being thought about as they are asked to consider the needs of the children.

In this carefully planned space for talking and thinking, some of the staff's anxieties about the key person role described by Goldschmied and Jackson began to emerge. Two concerns in particular were prominent and are familiar from our experience in other nurseries:

Notes from a Development Team meeting

1. Challenges for the Senior Management Team (SMT)

■ Managers need to revisit the allocation of paired key persons so as to cover annual leave, training and other reasons for absence. At present, the manager of the room is standing in as the second person. This works to some extent as she knows all the children, but it is unmanageable because there are days when too many children need her when their key person is away training or sick. It is also confusing for the children. We suggest that matched workers take on that role for emotional support and group work while the manager will be a back-up for organising activities and practical tasks not directly involving the children. This means that key persons and their groups will move on together in the centre, whereas the manager of the under-threes section will be staying to manage quality in that age group. So that means more consistency for children and key persons if matched key persons progress through the centre.

■ We feel strongly that each member of staff should be trusted to be a key person and that each key person is inducted and trained for her special role. The key person role is taken by every member of staff, not only the most gregarious, or the member of staff who happens to be of a similar ethnic background to a particular family, or appears to be in tune with a particular child-rearing style. We think it is important that each key person is supported to take that role with her group of children, and that no one is pressurised to admit children earlier if things are difficult at home. Some families may try and pressurise us because they do not understand how we are trying to implement settling in. This is an important point for Kittan's mother and grandma, as Kittan will be joining the nursery soon. Have we translated the settling-in policy booklet into Yoruba yet?

■ Please can the SMT check new admissions to accommodate part-time and full-time places. At the moment, Josie [key person] has too many children in her group on Wednesday morning. Tania [manager] is helping out and the ratio is OK but it is a bit hectic with so many part-time places that morning. Some of Josie's key children became distressed when she did not have time to greet them as 'individually' as on other mornings.

■ There is an issue with Kamlesh. Her father wants Sakina to be her key person as they both speak Punjabi/Urdu. We don't think that is going to be possible at the moment – Sakina already has a full group of children with a Pakistani background. Do we really want to give parents that kind of choice? Is that in line with our Equal Opportunities policy? After all we have agreed that *all* staff are entitled to professional opportunities and should have responsibilities for families from *all* kinds of minority and majority ethnic backgrounds. All key persons need to be trained and supported to be able to work with any family, not only the ones who may speak the same home language or practise the same religion as them. Please can we talk that through at the next staff meeting?

FIGURE 3.3 Building the key person approach in the Nursery Centre

There are lots of cultural sensitivities as well as professional issues we need to address here. No one should be passed over as a key person – that isn't fair. Just because Paula is a Rastafarian does not mean that she is not professionally competent to be a key person for Kamlesh. Kamlesh's parents might not choose Paula at first because she looks different to them, but we know she will do a good job in caring for children from families that are different from her own.

■ Things are going much better now that each key person has only one new child to settle in at a time. Settling in is stressful for the key person as well as for the child. It takes time and support from all of us. The SMT has staggered admissions to ensure that every child and family can go through the settling-in programme without being rushed. The SMT also needs to ensure that the new information booklet will explain this staggered admissions system to all the parents . . . and to grandparents too! They can put pressure on the nursery staff to admit children early when things are difficult at home.

2. Language and terminology

Please can we remind everyone that it is essential to be precise about the words we use and what they mean for us, for example 'key nursery groups', and NOT 'family groups'. We think it is important to be clear that we are NOT the children's family, or trying to replicate that in any way. The key person nursery groups in the Centre are different kinds of attachment networks from those at home.

3. Practical activities to 'bond' key nursery groups and their key person together

These are special and personal activities created by each key person for 'her' children and their families, for example:

■ nursery group photograph albums;

■ 'message boxes' for children to leave gifts, objects and toys for each other;

■ 'coffee' mornings and picnic days for key group families so that each family can get to know the others with whom they share a key person;

■ 'gift boxes', opened at nursery group times, which contain objects from the key person to 'her children'; for example, autumn leaves, all of which are different but specially selected to enhance their sense of belonging to a special group;

■ a collection of small purses, bags or boxes containing different things including personal things from home;

■ Aziza is going back to Pakistan for a few months to mourn with her family after the death of her grandfather. We think it is important to prepare her and the others in her key group for her short absence. How shall we find rituals to say goodbye to children who are leaving the key group, or to welcome them back after an absence of some weeks? We have agreed to e-mail her auntie in Pakistan with messages for her and her mother to keep in touch and sustain their sense of belonging to the group here.

FIGURE 3.3 continued

- Being called a 'key person' not only raises parents' expectations of what this role might mean but also propagates the fear of not being able to fulfil it.
- The impossibility for key persons to be with 'their key children' all of the time.

Interestingly, the owner/manager described how a few of the parents were familiar with the term 'key person' and responded very enthusiastically to the idea of having one for their child. Naturally, some staff became anxious about what parents might come to expect, and whether they could or should be trying to meet these expectations. This nursery had not done any preparatory work with parents and felt, with hindsight, that it would have helped to ensure that parents and staff had matching hopes, if only to reduce some of the fears about overwhelming expectations.

What is the basis for the second anxiety though? Goldschmied and Jackson never suggest that a key person could or even should be with their key children all the time! Not even a parent can manage this. And if they did, how would a child begin to learn that, while separations might always be at least a little painful, they do allow the possibility of forming new relationships and that the loved person does return?

Perhaps, based on these anxieties, the staff chose to use the term 'special person' rather than 'key person', arguing that it expressed more directly what the role meant for them. Taking the trouble to ensure there is an adult who is designated 'special person' to a child has the effect of making that child feel special. This matters most of all at the beginning of the day when children arrive at nursery. For new children, particularly the youngest who are often coping with separation as a new experience, this may be the time when they most feel they are not special enough and that is why they have been left by their parents. This nursery has a policy that one member of staff is designated each day to be by the door so that every child and parent is greeted individually. This policy seemed particularly important as a platform on which to build the key person approach: from being greeted by 'someone' (*any* member of the staff) to being greeted by your special person (not just *any* member of staff, but a *particular* member of staff).

Over the last year in their new premises, the key person approach has grown, but with ebbs and flows. There are continual practical and logistical difficulties to solve, plus the normal human tendency to let working practices lapse. The manager allocates all children to an established member of staff (new members of staff are given time to manage their own settling in before being asked to help children with settling in). But the matching process, undertaken by the deputy managers (involved in day-to-day dealings with the children and more likely to have a clearer insight into the children's individual needs than the manager), is logistically complex.

A first and most basic consideration is the need to ensure, as far as possible, that part-time staff are linked to children who attend nursery on corresponding days. Existing members of staff should not be allocated too many children; for the role of key person to remain viable, the maximum number is perhaps five or six.

A second consideration has been the timing of admissions. Local authority and LEA-maintained nurseries may be able to delay admitting children until the appropriate key person is available to help them settle (see Example 2, above). For nurseries that have to perform an even tighter financial balancing act, delaying admissions may not be commercially possible.

And thirdly, there are the inevitable preferences of human nature. We have already emphasised our belief that all professional staff should be able and prepared to work with any parent. This remains an important principle. But sometimes, children or parents do 'click' strongly with a particular member of staff on the basis of some shared background or experience, or perhaps just because that is the way human beings are.

The nursery in this example starts the key person relationship with a two-week settling-in period. The first week, the parent stays with their child. The key person concentrates on getting to know the child and family and aims to help them become familiar with the nursery. During the second week, parent and key person can begin to plan graduated times for leaving the child. It is so easy to underestimate the sophistication of this professional work by the key person. She will draw on her knowledge and training as well as on her personal experience of coping with partings and reunions. And parents have widely differing feelings and ways of coping with the intrinsic difficulty of handing the care of their child to someone else. They have different external demands too and some will be under much greater pressure than others to hurry through this period. While parents and the key person often start to build a powerful bond during this time, they will not always be comfortable partners or 'of one mind' about how to manage the details of this settling-in process.

One parent complained that her designated 'key person' was not often available to speak to her. When the manager raised this with the worker, she explained how intimidating she found the parent and recognised that, while she was working very closely with the child, she did tend to avoid the parent.

How does a manager respond to this basic block to building an effective partnership? She has to make a judgement about whether this is a difficulty that she can help the member of staff manage, as part of the staff member's own growth and development, or whether that is unrealistic at that particular time. On this occasion, the owner/manager decided to switch key persons while being careful to make it a learning rather than a negative experience for the staff member concerned.

We believe this key person 'switching' should be very much a last resort. If the key person approach is to be understood as a way of building close professional relationships between the worker, child and family, this must be recognised as a sophisticated task that will entail challenges and uncertainties, as well as learning new skills of interacting with parents – parents whose social or cultural background may differ greatly from the key person's. The professional development of the key person depends on these challenges being addressed and worked at. Changing the key person may limit the opportunity for this professional development to take place.

The intimidation can work the other way too. Another parent was visibly anxious about being in the nursery. Yet the link between her and her child's key person has proved immensely positive. When the key person commented on how much the child had grown in confidence, his mother commented 'I have too!' We should not underestimate the potential benefits that a successful key person relationship can bring to the whole family.

Aiding professional growth

There is a crucial point here about the management role of taking account of individual staff members' professional growth and maturity. Each member of staff must be involved in the key person approach; however, key relationships are complex and the development of the key person approach must go hand in hand with the growth and development of individual members of staff. The owner/manager of the nursery in Example 3 said some members of staff might find it hard to understand the importance of close tactile experiences for children needing comfort; others struggle to see tears and distress as an expression of real pain or grief rather than a child 'being difficult'.

Encouraging individually distinct relationships in nursery means staff have to cope with their own painful feelings of change and loss. A little boy wanted to 'move away' from his key person in order to spend more time exploring and being with other adults and children. The key person was hurt: 'He doesn't love or need me any more.' The owner/manager of Nursery three felt she had to try to understand and discuss her employee's feelings rather than label the staff member as 'unprofessional' or 'possessive'. Another child, having become confident and independent, regressed when his baby sister was born, returning to a stage of wanting greater closeness to and attention from his key person. His key person understood what was happening and responded positively.

How do parents respond to these obviously important relationships their children make with other adults? In one way, their responses and reactions are as variable as those of the staff. Overall though, parents seem to be relieved that there is a 'special person' for them and their child. Perhaps they chose a particular nursery precisely because of its underpinning philosophy? Other nurseries that have not taken a key person approach, either implicitly or explicitly, may need to work much more with parents before introducing it. Nevertheless, when parents are in the setting the owner/manager of Nursery three continually reminds staff of the basic ground rule that *the parents are the parents and the staff are not,* and she emphasises that parents should be the main carers and staff must take a supporting role.

The key person approach is not an easy option. But the nurseries in Example 1–3 demonstrate that it can be managed, and highlight, in practice, its highly significant benefits to children and parents.

The key person approach: essential elements of the role

One way of making the role of key person explicit is to write a 'job description' – an effective way of setting out key responsibilities and bringing into sharp focus the division between what, wherever possible, the key person should do, and activities that remain team responsibilities. In one nursery, a member of staff said 'We are all key people – we all matter'. Of course this is true; the whole staff team will retain a collective responsibility for all the children in the nursery.

But nurseries should outline the specific responsibilities of the key person for particular children. This does not mean that team-working is abandoned; rather that team relationships are developed. It takes a considerable degree of support and trust for each member of staff to know when to hold back from responding to or doing something for a child, allowing the key person to fulfil this role instead. A nursery staff team might adapt the list of responsibilities listed in Figure 3.4.

Figure 3.4 contains an important list of the basic responsibilities of the key person role. In the following case study, a practitioner shows her reflection and thoughtfulness about the point listed in Figure 3.4: *'Eating with your key children in small key groups'* and how to translate this into the reality of day-to-day interactions (Randolph Beresford Centre 1999).

- Developing secure trusting relationships with your key children and parents.

- Interacting with your key children with reciprocal sounds, words, facial expressions and gestures, according to their individual temperament.

- Providing a secure base for your key children by supporting their interests and explorations away from you. Perhaps by smiling and nodding as they explore and by drawing their attention to interesting things around them.

- Providing a secure base for your key children by being physically and emotionally available to them to come back to, by sitting at their level and in close proximity to them.

- Using body language, eye contact and voice tone to indicate that you are available and interested, gauging these according to the child's temperament and culture.

- Understanding and containing children's difficult feelings by gentle holding, providing words for feelings and empathy in a way suited to each individual child.

- Comforting distressed children by acknowledging their feelings, offering explanations and reassurances calmly and gently.

- Acknowledging and allowing children to express a range of feelings, anger, joy, distress, excitement, jealousy, love.

- Settling new key children into the setting gradually.

- Settling your key children as they arrive each day.

- Eating with your key children in small key groups.

- Holding key children who are bottle-fed on your lap to feed, maintaining eye contact and conversations.

- Changing and toileting your key children, using sensitive handling and familiar words.

- Dressing and washing your key children, offering help as needed but also supporting their growing skills.

- Having regular opportunities to reflect on the emotional aspects of key working with a skilled, knowledgeable manager or colleague.

Together these elements constitute key working.

FIGURE 3.4 Important aspects of a key person relationship (Manning Morton and Thorpe 2001: section 2, p. 9)

Case Study | **Reflections on the key person role**

I have thought about keeping boundaries for my key person role at lunchtime. I try to keep my voice calm; I try to be controlled, to be the big person, the adult for the child, to have empathy for the child. I have been reading about family relationships – that has been helpful. The book describes *'how children push the walls out to see if the roof will come down on their heads'.*

I try to make the walls/boundaries strong for them, so that the roof doesn't fall in, so the children feel safe with me as a strong adult.

I think mealtimes work best when the children are in a small group with their key person, so that they can have conversations, really talk together, not just be given instructions about what or how to eat or behave.

I am bothered about how we do that at mealtimes. Am I imposing my own ideas of good manners, or setting a pattern for conversations at mealtimes that may be very different from how things are at home for these children?

At home parents may be busy with cooking. Here Bronagh brings everything in for us, is it right that we teach our children our way (culture/family style or values), or should we think about other ways more matched to their home lives?

Mealtimes can be difficult, noisy, chaotic . . . that can be hard for the children. Callum likes to play under the table, Honeybee wants to push her chair in and out, their jokes together can get out of hand, too noisy for me but they are having a good time playing with one another . . .

Employers supporting the key person approach

Working with local employer groups in preparing to implement the key person approach can be fruitful. Can employers be encouraged to establish sympathetic work/life balance policies that allow for flexibility, so that settling-in times for children and breastfeeding arrangements are accommodated, and the 'triangle of trust' between parents, key person and child is established and sustained? There are encouraging signs that this is the case, even at very senior levels:

> Suma Chakrabarti, who next month becomes permanent secretary at the Department for International Development, has agreed with the secretary of state, Clare Short, that he will work from 9.30 a.m. to 5.30 p.m. five days a week. The arrangement also allows the first permanent secretary to spend every Friday at home to allow him to attend morning assembly at his daughter's school.
>
> (*Guardian*, 15 January 2002)

How can parents 'give themselves' to this settling-in time – with all the emotions it can arouse – if they also feel under pressure to get to work on time? You cannot give your best at work if leaving your child has been such a hurried affair that much of the rest of the day is spent worrying about how he or she is coping.

There may also be pressure from *within* the nursery to accelerate this settling-in time. Commercially run nurseries are, understandably, concerned with making nursery a flexible service for potential parent customers. As previously mentioned, talking to parents about being available and flexible during a settling-in period for their child may seem both a nuisance and an unnecessary complication. Such nurseries should recognise that they are promoting a quality service attuned for children and parents through the key person approach. Establishing the key person approach as a 'selling point' should *underpin* rather than *undermine* the quality of the service.

Observing, noticing and not noticing

During a seminar discussion, a nursery manager described how difficult it was to staff her baby unit:

> *'Some of the girls say it is boring working with the babies – it's not like the three- and four-year-olds; babies don't do much and the day passes so slowly.'*

When there is so much evidence of the rapidity of growth and development in the first months and years, how can it be that babies might be perceived as uninteresting to the point of being boring? Parents and close relatives take such obvious delight in their baby's new gestures, facial expressions or vocalisation. Why then is this not mirrored by the experience of staff in baby rooms?

We think that at least part of the reason that practitioners feel threatened is precisely because babies are so engaging and have such a powerful capacity to delight. Caring for a baby means involvement, being drawn into a relationship and responding to the child. Connection and affection cannot grow without the risk of pain and loss when the baby or toddler, inevitably, moves on. So staff may avoid this involvement by not allowing themselves to notice the baby's overtures.

There is a second reason for 'not noticing'. While much of what a baby communicates may be obvious and delightful, the complete opposite often also applies. The meaning of a baby's piercing cries or expressions of bewilderment may take time to interpret – what precisely is it that is so upsetting to the baby? It is completely understandable to want to stop this distress. The sometimes frantic efforts of nursery practitioners to distract babies and young children from their feelings by jiggling them up and down or showing them toys or mobiles are good examples of an inability to notice and think about what is really being communicated. The primary goal seems to be to stop the communication rather than understand it. The challenge of detailed 'noticing' is described by Margaret Rustin (1989: 20–1):

> ...to be a good observer...requires a space in the mind where thoughts can begin to take shape and where confused experiences can be held in an inchoate form until their meaning becomes clearer. This kind of mental functioning requires a capacity to tolerate anxiety, uncertainty, discomfort, helplessness, a sense of bombardment.

When given 'permission' to begin to observe in this way, to record impressions and personal feelings without being immediately clear about their meaning or significance, practitioners expressed their delight at how much there was to see (Shropshire and Telford and Wrekin Early Years and Child Care Development Partnership 2000). The simple acknowledgement that practitioners do have feelings about what they do and what they see appears to remove some of the fear, allowing them to notice more.

This type of detailed observation requires concentration and concurrent recording and cannot be done while working alongside the children. Some nurseries have managed this by allowing a staff member working in one room to observe in another, perhaps for a 20-minute 'block' during the day. Other settings have released staff to take turns to observe within a team, an example of which are the Avranches Nursery Professional Development Sessions which were held 1999–2000 in Jersey, Channel Islands.

But however it is organised, the key person approach in action must be monitored and informed by focused, detailed, individual child observations.

Sharing and not sharing information

The key person approach makes it possible for carers to bring informed and detailed knowledge of a child to the discussion of observation material and to make the best sense of it.

When parents in one nursery were asked to share something significant about what their children did at nursery that day, some said that they did not know, but added that, in some ways, they felt they *could not really expect to know* (Elfer, forthcoming). They explain that having made the choice to place their child in nursery, inevitably, at least in part, they had given up that detailed knowledge of what their child did each day. It was as if the parents felt they could not have the best of both worlds – that is, having a job *and* knowing what their child was doing.

Why should parents feel excluded or exclude themselves in this way? Certainly there was no suggestion that the nurseries had been reluctant to share information. But the parents' *perception* that they were not really entitled to it does highlight the role of the key person in taking the initiative to build a positive relationship, to offer information and to make clear the

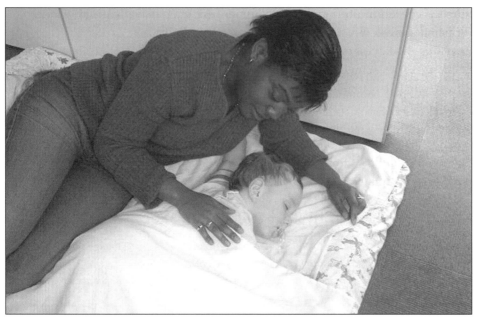

The key person settles the child to sleep. She pats him gently on his back. This is what his mother says he needs in order to drift off to sleep. With his hand he rubs the key person's woolly jumper and he sucks gently on his dummy – both comforting sensations that help him feel safe enough to sleep.

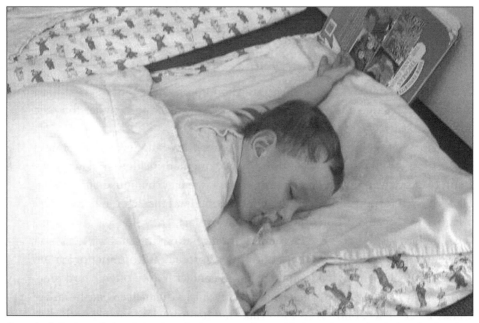

Once the baby is settled and sleeping, the key person leaves his favourite storybook close by for when he awakes. The baby is lying on his own special blanket from home so that the smells and associations of home may comfort and calm him.

nursery's need for information from home. Taking a passive role and waiting for parents to ask will not be enough for some parents.

Where the key person is not on duty when parents arrive to collect their child, nurseries sometimes use very simple devices to pass on information: 'Please remember to tell Daniel's parents that today, he did X and Y.' Liam's parent (see page 35) was touched (and presumably reassured about the nursery's commitment to take note of the information she had passed on in the home visit) by the trouble Leon had gone to on Liam's behalf. A parent is likely to be similarly touched by the trouble taken to remind a colleague to pass on some detail of what Daniel had done.

Discussion in nursery teams reveals the dilemmas of what *not* to tell parents. The following is a typical piece of advice:

> 'When a child takes his first step, it's better to tell parents "She looks as though she is about to take her first step so look out for it at home." When they come to you in a week's time and say, "You were right, she has just taken her first step" you let them enjoy that privilege and do not say "Oh we saw that two weeks ago." '

This seems very sensitive, well-intentioned practice. But is it consistent with an honest and open relationship with parents? Or does it treat parents as if they are very vulnerable and have to be protected from what they probably know already?

Physical contact and closeness, abuse and boundaries

Babies and young children need holding, cuddling and lap time, all of which are the very essence of being in a relationship. The key person approach maximises this in so far as it incorporates more physical contact conducted mainly by the same adults, always arising out of the child's, rather than the adult's, needs.

Of course, it would be irresponsible to ignore the dangers of physical and sexual abuse. Thankfully, the number of documented incidents in nursery is small but the deep and long-lasting damage wreaked by abuse of any kind places a great responsibility on every practitioner and manager to be alert and sensitive to any suggestion of inappropriate contact.

Some local authorities are developing policies to guide practitioners – an important step in ensuring that children are protected from inappropriate contact, as well as from inadequate physical contact. We've often heard practitioners say *'Of course you're not allowed contact with children any more – it's the Children Act.'* The Children Act 1989 *does not* ban physical contact with children! Denying children physical comforting and holding would be as abusive to youngsters as imposing it for adults' gratification.

Many local authority policies seem to have struck a sensitive balance in placing physical touch at the centre of the 'curriculum' for babies and toddlers. Figure 3.5 provides a good example of this from St Stephen's Nursery Centre in East London.

It is important for children to see practitioners interacting and relating to each other in positive ways. In this nursery we positively encourage the staff and children to develop happy secure relations and play together. Our teaching through play policy includes the area of emotional development. The following details the ways in which personal relationships between adults/children are developed.

- Through physical contact, such as holding children's hands.
- Holding children gently to reassure them.
- Cuddling children to express delight in their behaviour.
- Tickling them, to gain attention, to respond to their attempts at communication.
- To laugh with children when they show excitement, discovery and pleasure in the world.
- To smile, make funny faces.
- To sit children on your lap, give comfort to them when they are upset and help them to achieve a goal.
- To talk about things that can make children and adults happy or sad.

FIGURE 3.5 Example of nursery guidelines on physical touch and holding

---

People sometimes object to men taking on the role of key person. But some early years settings have taken a very positive approach not only to the need for more men to be working as early childhood professionals, but also for them to take a full part in the care of the youngest children:

> Parents have at various times expressed misgivings about men giving intimate care (nappy changing, toileting children etc.) and also put forward more general objections based on ideas of men taking away women's power by moving into the work. These objections have been met by establishing and publicising a witnessing policy, whereby workers do not give intimate care alone but work together, and by pointing out to the parents that if gender equality is achieved it will be because each gender is willing to give up its area of sole control. Some exceptions have been made in the area of intimate care for some parents – almost invariably for cultural or religious reasons.
>
> (Bateman 1998: 164)

A nursery policy on physical contact as set out in Figure 3.5, perhaps within the context of a wider philosophy as set out in the extract above, needs to be part of the 'infrastructure' of building the key person approach. (For further guidance, see 'References and further reading' at the end of this book.)

Mentoring and supervision

A nursery key person having support and supervision. The nursery manager plans in regular times when staff with responsibilities for particular children have time to talk, so as to develop their work with the children and their families. The supervisor also introduces the key person to relevant reading material to support her professional development.

The key person approach does bring staff closer to children and children closer to staff. Relationships are more sensitive and responsive, observations of children more detailed, and home–nursery links more interactive. It would be irresponsible to allow, never mind encourage, this to happen without a system of checks and balances to ensure that professional boundaries are maintained and practice is clearly accountable within the nursery-management system. As staff become more involved with the children, more emotional demands will be placed on them:

> However, the nursery nurses' increased affection for the infants also made them more distressed about the inadequacy of parenting which some of the infants received. Two young nursery staff spoke of spending sleepless weekends worrying about the happiness and safety of 'their' babies. Commitment to these disadvantaged infants was achieved at considerable emotional cost.
>
> (Hopkins 1988: 106)

And, as the views in Figure 3.6 illustrate, there are many other sources of emotions to manage.

Boundaries between professional and parental roles may occasionally become confused. Mentoring and supervision is an essential tool for keeping these relationships under systematic review and is recognised as a complex but crucial element in all professional roles working in a caring or helping way with others:

Other people's

'It is hard dealing with the children who cling on. My key child won't let me go anywhere without her. It is wearing me out.'
(A key person speaks about a child who is taking a long time to settle)

'I didn't know what to do when a grandma came in in tears and pleaded with me to admit her child early because of the difficult circumstances in her family. I wanted to help but I already had a full group of key children and nobody else had space at the time. What do you do when people are so upset?'
(A key person describes the struggle to cope with the anxiety and distress of others)

Dealing with fears

'It is difficult when little Honeybee goes to Zillah for comfort. I am her key person. I feel upset that she doesn't want me and does not seek me out. I think that Zillah should pass Honeybee over to me and help me form a relationship with her. If Zillah cuddles her, she is distracted away from being with her own key children and then how am I going to form a special relationship with her?'
(A key person having difficulty establishing a relationship with her key child describes her feelings of jealousy and anger at a colleague's lack of support)

Our own

FIGURE 3.6 Dealing with feelings

As supervisors, you have to encompass many functions in your role. In part you are a counsellor giving support; you are also an educator helping the supervisee learning and developing; and in many situations, you are also a manager with responsibilities both for what your supervisee is doing and also to the organisation within which you both work. Several writers have looked at the complexity of roles that this provides for supervisors. Sub-roles most often noted are:

Teacher	Colleague
Monitor/evaluator	Boss
Counsellor	Expert technician.

(Hawkins and Shohet 1989: 37–8)

Margy Whalley (1996: 170) has also highlighted the importance of supervision in early years settings:

> It would not have been possible for staff to remain open to criticism and to appraise their own work critically if they had not received consistent supervision. We set up a system where most staff receive supervision/support every three weeks from a senior member of staff. Senior staff then receive support from the Head of Centre who in turn has a monthly consultancy session with an external consultant (a lecturer in the University social work department). This level of supervision is essential for staff working in a centre for under-fives which combines a social work and educative role working as a team.

An example of why such regular and systematic review is necessary is given in the following case study.

Case Study   **Keeping professional boundaries accountable and under review**

'Beginnings' is a private nursery in a rural part of the Midlands. The nursery has been developing its key person approach for a year and each member of staff has responsibility for a small group of children of mixed ages. One of Kevin's key children is Jack who is 18 months. Jack arrived in nursery one morning apparently quite well but, by lunchtime, staff were concerned that he appeared unwell and when they took his temperature, it was nearly 100°F. Kevin phoned Jack's mother and she agreed to leave work and collect Jack. When she arrived nearly an hour later, Jack's temperature had gone up a little further. Jack seemed pleased and relieved to see his mother and she took him home, saying she might take Jack to the doctor. During the remainder of his shift, Kevin phoned Jack's mother twice to see how he was. He also phoned from home in the evening to see what the doctor had said. Next day, Jack's mother asked to speak to the nursery manager. She said she did not want to seem unappreciative of the care Kevin had taken but she felt his phone call the previous evening had been a 'bit over the top'. She felt her care of Jack was being checked up on.

It does seem as if Kevin has allowed his professional relationship with Jack and Jack's parents to become blurred, and that while his phone calls may have been very well intentioned, Jack's mother experienced them as inappropriate and intrusive. It is a good example of why we emphasise that it would be irresponsible to implement a key person approach without the checks and monitoring provided by a supervision and mentoring system.

Some nurseries are already implementing a mentoring system effectively while others are beginning to build it into nursery budgets as an essential cost. In the case study below, Helen Watson (2002; personal communication with authors) describes, from a practitioner's point of view, just how integral the mentoring and supervision process is considered to be within an early years family centre.

Case Study | **Supervision and mentoring**

I wasn't familiar with supervision until I came to work at Netherton Park Family Centre as a seconded deputy. Previously I'd worked as an Early Years Coordinator in a school in a very challenging area of Birmingham where there was a desperate – and unmet – need for the opportunity to reflect on children and issues of concern in *regular*, carefully managed, confidential professional meetings. At Netherton Park, members of the staff team (secretaries, nursery nurses, teachers, students, project manager and deputies) have, at least, a monthly two-hour meeting with their line manager. This is seen as so valuable that nothing is allowed to compromise it – in the rare circumstances that a meeting has to be cancelled it is immediately rescheduled.

Although certain aspects, like discussion of children who are on either the Special Needs Register or the Child Protection register form part of every month's agenda, there is also scope to focus on areas identified by either the worker or the line manager. We use this forum to look at issues like relationships with other staff members, children and parents, areas for development and, if needed, it's the opportunity to have a good grumble about anything and everything to do with work.

The supervisors are carefully trained in a range of supervision and counselling techniques and there is a negotiated contract (including a complaints procedure). Because of its obvious impact on self-esteem and sense of personal worth, the process plays a vital part in the good working relationships between staff, parents and children and it can have a therapeutic role. For example, in supervision recently it allowed us to reach some understanding of a parent of a child who was born with quite complex needs. The mother found it very difficult to cope with her child's growing independence and she clearly experienced jealousy of staff at the Centre for the part they played in developing the child's skills. Supervision helped the child's key worker, who was understandably upset at the occasional hostile outbreaks of the parent, to put it into some framework and not to take it personally whilst developing strategies to communicate with the family.

We also have group supervisions – which we try to have off-site (usually in a local pub) – where all staff involved in the nursery part of the Family Centre have an opportunity to discuss a range of common issues and to share useful information. These are very honest discussions and there appears to be little that would come under the heading of a 'no-go area'.

Supervision (which should not be confused with appraisal or staff meeting) in my experience has a wholly positive effect on the well-being of the team. In turn, this impacts on the life of the Centre and the relationships we have with children and parents.

A supervision system should be seen as essential, in *every* early years setting. This is first and foremost to ensure professional boundaries are retained and that all relationships are accountable within the quality assurance processes of the nursery. But secondly, staff have a right and entitlement to this regular and trained support in recognition of the complex and sophisticated work they are asked to do with children and families.

The key person approach: what would you look for?

Thinking about the details of the key person approach

NATIONAL STANDARDS OF CARE of young children (under the age of 8), outside the family home, are set by the government under the Children Act 1989 as amended by the Care Services Act 2000. There are 14 'National Standards' and each Standard has linked 'supporting criteria', which set out how Ofsted inspectors will make judgements about how well that Standard is being met.

The government has also published guidance to accompany the Standards and to help providers of day care understand what is expected by each Standard (Ofsted 2001). This guidance has been drawn up in consultation with organisations representing the main providers of day care, for example the National Day Nurseries Association, Pre-School Learning Alliance, National Childminding Association and the Kids Clubs Network.

While the 14 Standards are the same for all types of day care, the government has published five sets of guidance to take account of the particular circumstances and aims of different types of day care. The five sets cover:

- Full day care
- Sessional day care
- Childminding
- Crèches
- Out-of-school clubs.

Each set of guidance describes 'outcomes' that providers should aim to achieve. The Standards represent a baseline of quality below which no provider should fall. The Standards are also intended to underpin a continuous improvement in quality in all settings.

Throughout the guidance, there are references to the key person approach:

- **Guidance for Standard 2 – Organisation:** *'The key person coordinates information about the individual child's needs and development and shares this with parents and other workers to maintain consistency and continuity of care.*

They provide a vital link with parents and carers and are often crucial in settling children into the setting. The role may also include coordinating the planning and record-keeping for individual children' (ibid.: 12).

- **Guidance for Standard 9 – Equal Opportunities:** *'Think about using the key person system to gain information from parents regarding such matters as diet, special skin or hair care, special words, comforters, nappy-changing procedures, sleep routines, family names, religion, language, health and medical conditions, favourite toys and likes and dislikes'* (ibid.: 42).

- **Guidance for Standard 10 – Special Needs:** *'You and your staff need sensitivity and knowledge to work with children with special educational needs and their parents. Think about . . . the role of the key person'* (ibid.: 45).

- **Guidance for Standard 12 – Working in Partnership with Parents and Carers:** *'Exchanging information with parents can be achieved by regular discussions. You might also think about . . . using the key person system . . . in ensuring privacy and confidentiality, you will need to consider the role of the key person'* (ibid.: 51).

- **Guidance for Annex A – Babies and Children Under 2:** *'Staff working with babies should have suitable training and experience in caring for such young children. They offer continuity of care by suitable staffing arrangements and by consulting with parents about children's individual routines'* (ibid.: 61).

In November 2002, the government launched *Birth to Three Matters: A Framework to Support Children in Their Earliest Years*. This framework places the role of a key person, at home and in the nursery, as one of its core principles.

In the remainder of the chapter, we make some suggestions for how to think about the detail of setting up a key person system that builds on these references to the key person approach and reflects the spirit of the key person approach throughout the Standards. The suggestions are congruent with and augment the National Standards. These additional details match the purpose of the Standards for continuous dynamic improvement in quality practice and may support parents and staff in looking out for evidence of a key person approach in action.

In addition, the ideas below suggest what evidence to look for in a key person approach. By checking out or monitoring the quality of what is happening in the setting, practitioners and policy-makers may reflect and plan developments in the sophistication and quality of their key person approach.

The ideas set out in the following tables do not cover all the Standards – neither are they exhaustive or comprehensive within the Standards that are covered. They will, however, help you to begin to think about what a key person approach may really look like in practice.

STANDARD 1

Suitable Person: *Adults providing day care, looking after children or having unsupervised access to them are suitable to do so.*

Which features of the setting support the key person approach in relation to this Standard? *(Documented evidence may include planning, policies, and written observations)*	What can you look for? *(Observable evidence will be of children's experiences of the implementation of the Standard)*
■ The person in charge should have a minimum of three years' experience of group care to ensure that she/he has the relevant skills and experience to meet the standards and be able to demonstrate a year-by-year programme of commitment to an ongoing programme of staff development and training for the key person approach. ■ Dated evidence of *induction* into the setting-specific key person procedures is in place. This documented evidence will be recorded in the professional profile documents of all key persons responsible for the intimate physical care and day-by-day contact with children. ■ Dated records of regular *supervision* sessions for key persons show that opportunities are available for the key person to talk about concerns and significant learning episodes of the key children in her/his group with a person in charge who is professionally qualified for that responsibility (see section 1.4 of the guidance).	For this standard, all of the relevant evidence will be documentary rather than observable practice.

STANDARD 2

Organisation: *The registered person meets required adult–child ratios, ensures that training and qualifications requirements are met and organises space and resources to meet the children's needs effectively.*

Which features of the setting support the key person approach in relation to this Standard? *(Documented evidence may include planning, policies, and written observations)*	What can you look for? *(Observable evidence will be of children's experiences of the implementation of the Standard)*
■ Every child and their family will be allocated a key person to encourage continuity of care and communication between home and the setting. ■ The adult–child ratios relates to key person time available to work directly with children and their families. ■ Additional staff and management time will be required for training, and for support of key practitioners, to prepare meals, for domestic tasks, and for maintenance of premises and equipment (in addition to the time spent with children). ■ Rotas, holiday schedules, and training programmes account for key persons' time being managed. This is to try to ensure that paired key persons are not on annual leave or training at the same time, so that children have a consistent key person or the 'paired back-up' key person working with them and their family. This operational plan will have evidence of regular review and updating. ■ There is a setting-specific policy for settling-in new children and their families with their allocated key person. ■ Staff records include personal profiles of all training and ongoing professional development, with dated records of certificates of attendance for induction training, and for professional development in a key person approach. These records should show that staff have had recent and relevant professional development work on a key person approach.	■ Children and families are greeted, and children are reunited with their home carers by one of their (paired) key persons. ■ Children's intimate physical care (nappies, bottle feeding, care when injured or sick) is mostly carried out by key persons. ■ Children spend regular and frequent episodes of activity, not merely fleeting contact, during the day in small key person groups. (As well as other times when children will have opportunities to be with other children and adults in other groups.) ■ Children and their families who are new to the setting are playing and communicating together during the settling-in process.

STANDARD 3

Care, Learning and Play: *The registered person meets children's individual needs and promotes their welfare. They plan and provide activities and play opportunities to develop children's emotional, physical, social and intellectual capabilities.*

Which features of the setting support the key person approach in relation to this Standard? *(Documented evidence may include planning, policies, and written observations)*	What can you look for? *(Observable evidence will be of children's experiences of the implementation of the Standard)*
Records will be kept by key persons of: ■ Staff and parents' observations of what key children in their group can do. ■ The planning of what key persons will do to respond to these observations (see sections 3.3 and 3.9). ■ Each child's stepping stones of progress and development.	■ Children will be more likely to seek physical comfort and affection from their key person at times of uncertainty or stress. ■ Children will be in small family-type groups at greeting times and in a few other small group sessions at certain points in the day when key persons will talk and play with them. ■ Key persons will know and be able to use a few words in their key groups' home language(s) if children are bi/multilingual learners (for example, colloquial greetings, words for comforters or basic physical needs). ■ Children will be communicating and playing in their home languages as well as in English. Key persons will value this development and will know about the cultural identities, languages and religions of each child and his/her family in the key group. ■ Children may be being observed while they play by their key person who will be documenting what the child can do. (For example, the key person may be watching, listening, writing observations down, video recording, making entries in home/school diaries, etc.) ■ There will be groups of key practitioners and home carers having conversational exchanges. There will be times, spaces, and suitable adult furniture for parents and key persons to talk together about their child's play, care, and learning.

STANDARD 4

Physical Environment: *The premises are safe, secure and suitable for their purpose. They provide adequate space in an appropriate location, are welcoming to children and offer access to necessary facilities for a range of activities which promote their development.*

Which features of the setting support the key person approach in relation to this Standard? *(Documented evidence may include planning, policies, and written observations)*	What can you look for? *(Observable evidence will be of children's experiences of the implementation of the Standard)*
■ Where outdoor space adjoining the premises is not provided or is limited, suitable arrangements for physical activity and fresh air will be made as part of the child's daily experiences of care, play and learning in partnership with families and key persons. ■ There is an area where confidential information and necessary records can be kept and where managers or key persons may talk with parents confidentially.	■ Parents and key persons may have withdrawn to a private space to talk confidentially. ■ Key persons in a staffroom may be documenting children's learning and keeping records up to date, reading (professional journals, newspaper articles concerned with children and childhood, etc.), preparing activities or play materials to support and extend the children's observed interests ... as well as taking breaks for relaxation. ■ Children are sometimes engaged in home-like activities alongside their key person, for example folding clothes, arranging fruit on a plate for a snack to offer other children, visiting the local shop to buy food for the nursery rabbit, making food for a celebration, perhaps from produce the children may have grown in the nursery garden.

STANDARD 7

Health: *The registered person promotes the good health of children and takes positive steps to prevent the spread of infection and appropriate measures when they are ill.*

Which features of the setting support the key person approach in relation to this Standard? *(Documented evidence may include planning, policies, and written observations)*	What can you look for? *(Observable evidence will be of children's experiences of the implementation of the Standard)*
■ Key persons will link, and document plans, with other professionals and home carers to ensure continuity of treatment when children are ill or in need of day-by-day medical care. ■ Individual training for key persons may need to be provided for them to ensure continuity of health care with home carers. ■ Key persons (under supervision from managers) will document evidence of medicines or treatments. Records with times, dates, and a note of which person administered the medicine/massage/exercise (e.g. a nut allergy treated with an emergency injection of a phial of antidote; temperature taken; regular skin treatment administered with parent's choice of cream; exercises for a child with cerebral palsy, etc.). ■ Records of training/mentoring by a qualified health professional for key persons to learn the technical or medical knowledge needed to treat the children in their key groups – to ensure inclusion in the full life of the nursery as well as for monitoring and reviewing any treatments with parents and link health professionals.	■ Children being treated by their key person who is knowledgeable about the treatment and the methods for administering it for the key children in her group. ■ Children being nursed and supported when they are being treated by key persons who know their routines and the most comforting ways to acknowledge their fears or hurt (e.g. reciting a familiar rhyme learned at home to accompany the deep breaths while offering their 'puffa' to treat asthma; rocking a baby with pyrexia in a way known to comfort him, etc.). ■ Children will have free flow access to the outside as well as activities inside. Key persons will ensure that children have suitable clothing available for all kinds of weather. Key persons will be watching that the children in their group have an adequate balance between indoor and outdoor play and that they get enough rest and exercise. ■ Children will be eating snacks prepared for them, and food they have cooked and prepared for themselves.

STANDARD 7 continued

Health: *The registered person promotes the good health of children and takes positive steps to prevent the spread of infection and appropriate measures when they are ill.*

Which features of the setting support the key person approach in relation to this Standard? *(Documented evidence may include planning, policies, and written observations)*	What can you look for? *(Observable evidence will be of children's experiences of the implementation of the Standard)*
	■ Key persons will prepare snacks *for* the children, as well as cooking and preparing food *with* the children to teach them about healthy eating and a varied diet. All staff will be involved in these activities but the key persons will ensure that food matches each child's preferences, the personal and family dietary requirements, as well as encouraging their children to try new and different foods from the ones that may be familiar to them at home. Key persons will be reporting to parents at the end of the session the new food experiences of the children, and sharing their ideas of healthy eating with the families. Many families may have strong views so the key persons should keep these in mind in sustaining healthy eating habits being established at home. ■ Children taking a nap will be being settled by a key person who knows the personal style in which their child likes to settle to sleep. Examples include: 1 With a lullaby tape of their father's voice: 'Ya sim ya sim siyu sing sing, Ya four ya four leong jing jing' 'Twinkle, twinkle little star' sounds a bit like this in Cantonese. 2 Rubbing a child's back 3 Turning on the rotating mechanism on a mobile 4 Leaving briskly after arranging darkness and silence (Baz *et al.* 1997).

STANDARD 8

Food and Drink: *Children are provided with regular drinks and food in adequate quantities for their needs. Food and drink are properly prepared, nutritious and comply with dietary and religious requirements.*

Which features of the setting support the key person approach in relation to this Standard? *(Documented evidence may include planning, policies, and written observations)*	What can you look for? *(Observable evidence will be of children's experiences of the implementation of the Standard)*
■ Key persons obtain and keep records of information from parents about individual children's dietary health requirements, including food allergies, and take heed of them. ■ Key persons obtain and keep records of information from parents about individual children's culinary cultural background so that familiar food is included in their diets. This is so that food may contribute to a child's sense of continuity to home, as well as belonging to the setting. Serving familiar foods and adopting familiar ways of eating will contribute to treating each child with equal concern, and will show that their home meals are valued. ■ Details of a child's dietary requirements and food allergies will be recorded. ■ Details of food familiar to the child and of their cultural culinary background are recorded.	■ Babies being bottle-fed will be cradled by their key persons. A key person will be sitting in a comfortable supporting seat in a space that enables them to attend to the baby's cues for attention, digestion, or 'conversational' exchanges. ■ Breastfeeding mothers will be encouraged and supported to visit the nursery. Key persons may be alongside them to learn the baby's individual style of feeding and holding. ■ Children will be offered food and drink that matches the documented health and cultural requirements. Key persons will be ensuring that other staff, students, or voluntary helpers know about these requirements. ■ The key person will ensure the food and the methods of eating it are congruent with the cultural traditions of the families and staff in each setting/group. ■ The key person will ensure that equal status and value will be given to choices of foods and eating styles within the social etiquettes of the communities. ■ Key persons will be involved with children and their parents in planning menus (see sections 8.2, 8.3 and 8.4).

STANDARD 9

Equal Opportunities: *The registered person and staff actively promote equality of opportunity and anti-discriminatory practice for all children.*

Which features of the setting support the key person approach in relation to this Standard? *(Documented evidence may include planning, policies, and written observations)*	What can you look for? *(Observable evidence will be of children's experiences of the implementation of the Standard)*
See all other Standards and the guidance, pages 43–6, sections 10.6.7 and 10.7. ■ The EYCDP Equal Opportunities Coordinator will link with the key person to ensure all practices are anti-discriminatory and take account of recent legislation to ensure inclusive practices, for example Race Relations Amendment Act 2000 and the SEN and Disability Act 2001. ■ If a child is identified as a 'child in need' the manager ensures that the key person is trained, supervised and supported to give appropriate information to referring agencies after consultation with the child's parents. This is a cooperative task, with the SENCO taking the lead.	■ The key person liaises with parents to ensure that the children's records in his/her key group contain information that enables appropriate care, play and learning experiences to be planned for. ■ The key person ensures that she/he is able to liaise with families whose home language is not English by arranging for interpreters to assist with written, signed and spoken forms of communication. ■ The key person will ensure that some of the books, toys, play materials, labels and displays value the racial origin, religion, language and culture of the child's family. ■ Children are playing and communicating together in the many 'languages' of childhood, including exchanges in their home languages. ■ Children are choosing play materials that have similarities to, and differences from, their home environment. ■ Children seek out their key person when they need information or reassurance that springs from the key person who will have developed a professionally intimate relationship with their family.

STANDARD 10

Special Needs: *The registered person is aware that some children may have special needs and is proactive in ensuring that appropriate action can be taken when such a child is identified or admitted to the provision. Steps are taken to promote the welfare and development of the child within the setting in partnership with parents and other relevant parties.*

Which features of the setting support the key person approach in relation to this Standard? *(Documented evidence may include planning, policies, and written observations)*	What can you look for? *(Observable evidence will be of children's experiences of the implementation of the Standard)*
See all other Standards and the guidance, pages 43–6, sections 10.6. 7 and 10.7. ■ Arrangements should address the needs of the key person who will be the link person to other professionals concerned with the special needs of the child. ■ Managers in close consultation with key persons talk to parents about the need for any special services and equipment for the children in their care. ■ If a child is identified as a child in need the manager ensures that the key person is trained, supervised and supported to give appropriate information to referring agencies after consultation with the child's parents. ■ Disabled children or disabled parents will have the support they need to ensure that they have access to all the activities in the nursery and are able to participate in and contribute to the life of the nursery.	■ Children with disabilities or special educational needs will be supported by their key persons to have access to all the activities and play opportunities in the setting. ■ The key person will teach other children in the setting how they may take account of the special needs or impairments of the child to enable them to join in the play, or to ensure that the child may have the support, space or privacy for their interests. ■ The key person may be in a conversation with the early years SENCO who will be supporting her/him to develop skills in writing individual educational plans (IEPs).

STANDARD 11

Behaviour: *Adults caring for children in the provision are able to manage a wide range of children's behaviour in a way which promotes their welfare and development.*

Which features of the setting support the key person approach in relation to this Standard? *(Documented evidence may include planning, policies, and written observations)*	What can you look for? *(Observable evidence will be of children's experiences of the implementation of the Standard)*
See all other Standards and the guidance, pages 47–9. ■ There is a named member of staff within the setting who has the responsibility for overseeing how key persons work with their key children to resolve conflicts, and who has the skills, training and support, as well as access to expert advice if further support is necessary. ■ There is a policy for resolving conflicts and supporting children to develop pro-social behaviour within a key person approach which takes account of the particular knowledge and wishes of each child's family.	■ Adults working with children in the provision are working towards supporting their key children to manage their own conflicts and behaviour in a way that promotes their welfare and development. Key persons will have an important responsibility to match their responses to their key children and what they know, so as to take account of each child's maturity and development in a pro-social, non-violent manner. ■ Each child is being supported by key persons to resolve conflicts and develop pro-social behaviour. ■ Each child is supported by their key person to develop a sense of belonging to the group where they may contribute their own ideas and feelings, as well as to respect the ideas, feelings and wishes of the others in their group. ■ The key persons make opportunities to confirm to the child rules/conventions/manners of the group, as well as to challenge or change the agreed rules/routines/conventions of a group in a democratic and consultative moral ethos.

STANDARD 12

Working in Partnership with Parents and Carers: *The registered person and staff work in partnership with parents to meet the needs of the children, both individually and as a group. Information is shared.*

Which features of the setting support the key person approach in relation to this Standard? *(Documented evidence may include planning, policies, and written observations)*	What can you look for? *(Observable evidence will be of children's experiences of the implementation of the Standard)*
See all other Standards and the guidance, pages 50–3. ■ Information about activities provided for children is based on the shared observations of parents and key persons. ■ Documentation of observations, (written, videoed, or taped) of what children can do, and each child's progress is shared and contributed to by both the key person and the parents.	■ Parents are offering information, as well as asking about their child's learning in conversational exchanges at greeting and leaving times. ■ Key persons are offering and sharing information about their key children's learning at greeting and leaving times. Parents and key persons can also meet more formally during 'Open hours'. ■ Children are seen to move between, and seek out, their parents or key persons for affirmation, reassurance, shared episodes of exuberance, etc.

STANDARD 13

Child Protection: *The registered person complies with local child protection procedures approved by the Area Child Protection Committee and ensures that all adults working and looking after children in the provision are able to put the procedures into practice.*

Which features of the setting support the key person approach in relation to this Standard? *(Documented evidence may include planning, policies, and written observations)*	What can you look for? *(Observable evidence will be of children's experiences of the implementation of the Standard)*
■ Is there clear cross-referencing between the nursery child-protection policy and the role of the key person in collecting and coordinating accurate information about each child? ■ Guidance to the National Standards makes clear the importance of regular discussions with parents. An essential part of protecting children is to build as strong a relationship as possible with parents so that there is a good flow of information and they can feel as confident as possible to share any worries, stresses or concerns with the nursery. Is the importance of establishing this strong relationship with parents emphasised in the child-protection policy and evident in the kind of material included in planning and observation notes? ■ Does the nursery have a system for annual staff appraisal and/or staff supervision or mentoring to ensure each key person's professional relationship with each child is reviewed and maintained within clear professional boundaries? ■ Is it clear that if a member of staff had a concern or anxiety about the appropriateness of handling or physical contact of a child by the child's key person or any other member of staff, this should be discussed with a senior member of staff – primarily for the protection of the child but also to facilitate supervision and support for the member of staff?	■ Each key person is familiar with the nursery child-protection procedure and can describe how she/he systematically records observations of children's behaviour and well-being, collecting these from all members of staff who work with a child. ■ The key person can describe how such observations are shared with the nursery child-protection 'designated person' in the event of any concerns. ■ The key person can talk about relevant and appropriate details of each child's family background and current circumstances – showing evidence of regular communication and exchange of information between home and nursery – and use of this information is evident in individual planning for the child. ■ Observations of physical holding and handling of children by each member of staff show that this is for appropriate physical care, for example nappy changing and toileting; and that expressions of physical affection are in response to the needs of and overtures from children – that is, children reaching, asking, or seeking out physical closeness to their key persons. ■ Evidence of a culture of openness, debate, attention to children's assertiveness skills, and the involvement of parents. These are all factors that inhibit abuse. Key persons, male and female, will be part of warm and intimate responses to children's needs. These episodes of physical closeness will always be 'open', not behind closed doors or away from a group of staff working together. Staff peer-mentoring and critical teamwork will be evident in an inclusive approach to protection.

STANDARD 14

Documentation: *Records, policies and procedures are maintained, which are required for the efficient and safe management of the provision and to promote the welfare, care and learning of children. Records about individual children are shared with the child's parent.*

Which features of the setting support the key person approach in relation to this Standard? *(Documented evidence may include planning, policies, and written observations)*	What can you look for? *(Observable evidence will be of children's experiences of the implementation of the Standard)*
See all other Standards and the guidance, pages 57–62. ■ Records about individual children are kept confidential between those family and staff whom they concern. Some aspects will need to be confidential to just a few staff, while other records of learning, stepping stones of progress, and children's interests will be open to a wider professional team for planning curriculum and for staff development. Boundaries of confidentiality must be agreed between the parents, key persons and professionals involved.	You may observe key persons writing up a variety of records. They may be sitting among their key children, observing their play but not involved directly with their child-initiated activities. Their documenting could include: ■ Observations of children's play to inform planning of resources and activities. ■ Observations of play focusing on gathering evidence of stepping stones of progress towards development and learning to be noted in the child's profile of achievements. ■ Shared 'stories' of the child's experiences in the nursery to go to and fro from nursery to home, and from home back to the nursery (e.g. diaries, photographs, video tapes, etc.). ■ Notes for other professionals to enhance continuity and share information (e.g. physiotherapist, multi-lingual support practitioner, social worker supporting a family under stress, designated liaison person for child for protection, etc.). ■ Notes to go into the 'message boxes' for children (see point 3 in Figure 3.3 on page 43). ■ Reminder notes to families that they will be on a training course tomorrow and that (named person) will be the key person for their child while they are away. ■ A postcard for a child who is away in their group to keep them in touch and sustain their sense of belonging.

ANNEX A

Babies and Children Under 2: *These are additional criteria met by a registered person providing full day care who wishes to care for babies.*

Which features of the setting support the key person approach in relation to this Standard? *(Documented evidence may include planning, policies, and written observations)*	What can you look for? *(Observable evidence will be of children's experiences of the implementation of the Standard)*
See all other Standards and the guidance, pages 62–5. ■ Key persons ensure a secure emotional base for each child, and a special link with their families. ■ Babies are held while bottle-feeding, preferably by their key person. ■ Parents will need to know *who* changed their baby's nappy, and *who* offered a bottle to their baby. This is so that they can be reassured that the care is carried out by key persons or just a few adults with a close relationship to the child and the family. ■ It is unacceptable for babies' intimate physical care to be carried out by serial carers on a conveyor belt of duties for nappy changing of all the babies in the group. Students and temporary staff should not be responsible for the intimate care of babies. ■ There is clear planning for babies' activities based on the observations collated by the key person of their interests and preoccupations.	■ A baby will be in a small group with a key person. ■ A baby will reach for, call or cry for, or crawl towards the key persons with whom he/she has formed attachments. ■ A baby may protest when his/her key persons leave the room, which could be a healthy emotional response for a child with an attachment to his/her key person. ■ A baby will seek comfort, affirmation, or shared pleasure in experiences with his/her key adults and the other key children in his/her 'family' group. ■ A baby is likely to play and explore confidently and curiously when he/she is within sight or sound of his/her key persons.

References and further reading

Alvarez, A. (1992) *Live Company Psychoanalytic Psychotherapy with Autistic, Borderline, Deprived and Abused Children*. London: Routledge.

Bain, A. and Barnett, L. (1986) *The Design of a Day Care System in a Nursery Setting for Children Under Five*. London: The Tavistock Institute for Human Relations Occasional Paper, No. 8, p. 16.

Bateman, A. (1998) 'Child protection, risk and allegation', in Owen, C., Cameron, C. and Moss, P. (eds) *Men as Workers in Services for Young Children: Issues of a Mixed Gender Workforce*. Proceedings of a Seminar held at Henley on Thames, 29–31 May 1997. London: Institute of Education, University of London, 182–9.

Baz, P., Begm, L., Chia, K. *et al.* (1997) 'Working bilingually with early rhymes and poems', in Nutbrown, C. and Hannon, P. (eds) *Preparing for Early Literacy Education with Parents: A Professional Development Manual*. Nottingham: The REAL Project/NES Arnold.

Bonilauri, S. and Filipini, T. (1996) 'Messages Back and Forth', in Reggio Children *The Hundred Languages of Children: Narrative of the Possible*. Catalogue of the Exhibit. Washington, DC: Reggio Children.

Clark, A. and Moss, P. (2001) *Listening to Young Children: The Mosaic Approach*. York and London: Joseph Rowntree Foundation and National Children's Bureau.

Dahlberg, G., Moss, P. and Pence, A. (1999) *Beyond Quality in Early Childhood Education and Care: Postmodern Perspectives*. London: Falmer Press.

Dalli, C. (2000) 'Starting child care: what young children learn about relating to adults in the first weeks of starting child care', *Early Childhood Research and Practice* **2**(2).

Department for Education and Employment (DfEE) (1998) *National Childcare Strategy*. London: DfEE.

Department for Education and Skills (DfEE) (2000) Training Materials Introducing the QCA/DfES Guidance for the Foundation Stage Curriculum. London: DfEE.

Department for Education and Skills (DfES) (2002) *Birth to Three Matters: A Framework to Support Children in Their Earliest Years*. London: DfES.

de Zulueta, F. (1993) *From Pain to Violence: The Traumatic Roots of Destructiveness*. London: Whurr Publishers Ltd.

de Zulueta, F. (2001) Personal communication with authors.

Duffy, B. (2000) 'The key person in action at the Thomas Coram Early Excellence Centre'. Unpublished submission to Department for Education and Employment, October.

Elfer, P. (forthcoming) '5000 hours: organising for intimacy in the care of babies and children under three attending full time nursery'. Unpublished PhD thesis, University of Surrey. For more information, please contact Peter Elfer at Roehampton, University of Surrey.

Elfer, P. and Selleck, D. (1999) 'Children under three in nurseries: uncertainty as a creative factor in child observations', *European Early Childhood Research Journal*, **7**(1): 69–82.

Glover, L. and Glover, B. (2001) Personal communication with authors.

Goldschmied, E. and Hughes, A. (1982) *Infants at Work: Babies of 6–9 Months Exploring Everyday Objects*. London: National Children's Bureau (video).

Goldschmied, E. and Hughes, A. (1992) *Heuristic Play with Objects*. London: National Children's Bureau (video).

Goldschmied, E. and Jackson, S. (1994) *People Under Three: Young Children in Day Care*. London: Routledge.

Goldschmied, E. and Selleck, D. (1996) *Communication Between Babies in Their First Year*. London: National Children's Bureau (book and video).

Gopnik, A., Melzoff, A. and Kuhl, P. (1999) *How Babies Think: The Science of Childhood*. London: Weidenfeld and Nicolson.

Hawkins, P. and Shohet, R. (1989) *Supervision in the Helping Professions: An Individual, Group and Organisational Approach*. London: Open University Press.

Hay, S. (1996) *Special Issues in Nursery Management*. London: Baillière Tindall Ltd.

Hopkins, J. (1988) 'Facilitating the development of intimacy between nurses and infants in day nurseries', *Early Child Development and Care*, **33**: 99–111.

Karmiloff-Smith, A. (1995) *Baby It's You: The First Three Years*. Isle of Man: Beckmann Communication (video).

Leach, P. (1997) *Your Baby and Child: The Essential Guide for Every Parent*. London: Penguin.

McGurk, H., Caplan, M., Hennessy, E. and Moss, P. (1993) 'Controversy, theory and social context in contemporary day care research', *Journal of Child Psychology and Psychiatry*, **34**(1): 3–23.

Manning Morton, J. and Thorpe, K. (2001) *Key Times: A Framework for*

Developing High Quality Provision for Children Under Three Years Old. London Borough of Camden: Camden Early Years Under Threes Development Group.

Miller, L. (1992) *Understanding Your Baby*. London: Rosendale Press.

Miller, L., Rustin, M., Rustin, M. and Shuttleworth, J. (eds) (1989) *Closely Observed Infants*. London: Duckworth.

Ministry of Health and Ministry of Education (1945) *Nursery Provision for Children Under Five*. Circular 221/45. London: HMSO.

Mooney, A. and Munton, A. G. (1997) *Research and Policy in Early Childhood Services: Time for a New Agenda*. London: Institute of Education, University of London.

Munn, P. and Schaffer, H. R. (1993) 'Literacy and numeracy in social interactive contexts', *International Journal of Early Years Education*, **1**(3): 61–79.

National Children's Bureau (2002) *Everyday Stories – The Care and Learning of Children Under Three in Nursery*. London: National Children's Bureau Early Childhood Unit Archive.

National Institute of Child Health and Human Development Early Child Care Research Network (1997) 'The effect of infant child care on infant–mother attachment security: results of the NICHD study of early child care', *Child Development*, **68**(5): 860–79.

Office for Standards in Education (Ofsted) (2001) *Full Day Care: Guidance to the National Standards*. London: DfES.

Pen Green Centre (2002) *Growing Together*. Corby, Northants: Pen Green Centre (video).

Purvis, L. and Selleck, D. (1999) *Tuning In To Children: Understanding a Child's Development from Birth to Five Years*. A pocket book to accompany the BBC Radio 4 series. London: BBC Education.

Raikes, H. (1996) 'A secure base for babies: applying attachment concepts to the infant care setting', *Young Children*, **51**(5): 59–67.

Randolph Beresford Centre (1999) 'Unpublished working notes: the key person approach in practice'. London Borough of Hammersmith and Fulham. Available at the EYCDP Resource Base.

Roberts, R. (1995) *Self-Esteem and Successful Early Learning*. London: Hodder & Stoughton.

Robertson, J. and Robertson, J. (1989) *Separation and the Very Young*. London: Free Association Books.

Rustin, M. (1989) 'Introduction', in Miller, L., Rustin, M., Rustin, M. and Shuttleworth, J. (eds) *Closely Observed Infants*. London: Duckworth.

Ruth Forbes Jigsaw Nurseries (2001) 'Focus on mental health from birth through to primary school'. Presentation at a Study Day. London Borough of Hammersmith and Fulham Monday, 15 June.

Rutter, M. (1995) 'Clinical implications of attachment concepts: retrospect and prospect', *Journal of Child Psychology and Psychiatry*, **36**(4): 549–71.

St Stephens Nursery Education Centre (n.d.) *Learning and Teaching Through Play Policy*. London Borough of Newham.

Schaffer, H. R. (1998) *Making Decisions About Children: Psychological Questions and Answers*. Oxford: Blackwell.

Selleck, D. (2001) 'Being under three years of age', in Pugh, G. (ed.) *Contemporary Issues in the Early Years: Working Collaboratively for Children* (3rd edn). London: Paul Chapman Publishing, 78–95.

Shore, R. (1997) *Rethinking the Brain: New Insights into Early Development*. New York: Families and Work Institute.

Shropshire and Telford and Wrekin Early Years and Child Care Development Partnership (2000) 'Joint training initiative: staff development for baby and toddler observations in group care'. LEA internal publication, January.

Syal, M. (1997) *Anita and Me*. London: Flamingo.

Tobin, J., Wu, D. and Davidson, D. (1989) *Preschool in Three Cultures*. New Haven, CT: Yale University Press.

Trevarthen, C. (1998) Excerpt from an interview recorded for BBC Radio 4, in Purvis, L. and Selleck, D. (1999) *Tuning In To Children: Understanding a Child's Development from Birth to Five Years*. A pocket book to accompany the BBC Radio 4 series. London: BBC Education, 62.

Vernon, J. and Smith, C. (1994) *Day Nurseries at a Crossroads*. London: National Children's Bureau.

Watson, H. (2002) 'Report on practice at the Netherton Park Family Centre'. National Children's Homes Action for Children. Personal communication with authors.

Whalley, M. (1996) 'Working as a team', in Pugh, G. (ed.) *Contemporary Issues in the Early Years: Working Collaboratively for Children* (2nd edn). London: Paul Chapman Publishing, 170–88.

Winnicott, D. (1988) *Babies and Their Mothers*. London: Free Association Books.

Woodlands Park Nursery Centre (n.d.) *Information for Parents*. London Borough of Haringey.

Index

An 'f' after a page number indicates the inclusion of a figure; a 'p' after a page number indicates a photograph.

abuse 53
admissions 63
    limitations 49–50
    paced 38, 43f, 45
allocation 44–5
    spontaneity in, limitations 35–6
    switching 46
Alvarez, A. 9–10
apprehensions vi, 6–7, 24, 32–3, 56

babies 6, 19–20, 23, 50–1, 61, 75
    communication with 12–13, 14–16
    feeding 68
    interaction with 4–5p
    level of care 3–4
Bateman, A. 54
bereavement 43f
brain development, stimulation on 11
business focus 35
    large business 37–8, 39
    limitations 50
    medium-sized business 39–40, 42–3f
    small business 40–1, 44–6

child-centred practices 14, 23, 25p, 31, 43f, 52p, 73
child-protection policies 73
Children Act 1989 53
Clark, A. 31–2
commitment 18–19, 21, 26, 27
    statements on 30–1f
communication 12–13, 14–16, 20–1, 31–2, 33, 37–8, 42–3f, 64, 69
    limitations 50–1
    see also interaction; partnerships
community 9
confidence 21
confidentiality 65, 74
conflict management 71
consultants 30
continuing professional development 37, 38, 46–7, 55p, 56, 57, 58–9, 63

for health care 66
continuity of care 3–4, 11, 32, 39, 41, 42f, 44, 63
    see also separation
culture factors 36, 42–3f, 64
    diet 68
    see also Equal Opportunities
customer focus see business focus

Dahlberg, G. 7–8, 9
Dalli, C. 21–3
de Zulueta, F. 10–11
definitions 33
dependence, limitations 6, 7, 14–15, 16f, 56
diet 67, 68
Duffy, B. 26

emotional demands 27, 43f, 55–6f
empathy 15, 23, 31, 35, 46–7
Equal Opportunities 42f, 61, 69 see also culture factors
evaluation 30, 33, 42f
experience 62

fairness 32–3
families see parents
family-friendly practices 1, 2, 49–50
fathers see parents
food
    diet 67, 68
    mealtimes 48–9

government policies 1–2, 49
    Standards see Standards

Hawkins, P. 57
health care 66–8
holding
    communication as 12–13
    safety in 4p, 12, 14–15
home see parents
Hopkins, J. 32–3, 55

individual care 18, 44, 60–1, 63, 64, 75 see also individual terms
interaction 4–5p, 10, 12–13, 21–3 see also communication; partnerships

intrusion, perceived 57–8

Jackson, S. 10
job descriptions 47, 48f

knowledge 20, 25, 30, 35–6, 53, 72, 74
    limitations 51

Leach, P. 3
learning 19
life skills 49, 65
links *see* allocation

managers 32–3, 40–1, 42f, 44–6, 55p
Manning Morton, J. 35, 48f
mealtimes 48–9
mentoring 55, 56, 58 *see also* supervision
Miller, L. 12–13
Mooney, A. 3
morale 19, 26, 27
    limitations 50–1
Moss, P. 7–8, 9, 31–2
mothers *see* parents
Munton, A. G. 3

networks, as partnerships 8, 9, 13
noticing, limitations in 50–1
nutrition 67, 68

objections 7–9, 32
observation 23, 50–1, 64, 74
    of child-protection policies 73
outdoor activities 26p, 65

parents vi, 43f, 44, 45
    acting as 5–6, 8–9
    communication with 20, 21
    government policy on 1–2
    home–work commitments 1, 2, 49–50
    interaction with 4–5p
    mixed reactions from 24, 58–9
    partnerships with 18, 24, 25, 28, 35, 72, 73,
        75
    perceived marginalisation of 6–7, 51, 53,
        57–8
    as principal carers 6–8, 9, 20, 21, 22–3,
        26–7, 34, 35, 47
    social pressures on 1, 2
    visits to 20, 34, 35
partnerships 5, 21, 28, 35, 61, 72, 73, 75
    active 11–13, 15, 17f, 26p, 65
    discernment in 6, 12
    emotional demands from 27, 55–6f
    innateness of 9–10, 11
    limitations 6–9, 45–6, 56
    as networks 8, 9, 13
    special 10–11, 17, 18, 19–20, 24, 25, 40, 44,
        46–7
    see also communication; interaction
Pence, A. 7–8, 9
physical closeness 4p, 12, 14–15, 25p, 34p, 53,
    73

men and 54
    statements on 54–5f
play 26p

quality of care 2, 3, 11 *see also individual terms*

records 62, 63, 64, 65, 72
    on child-protection policies 73
    confidential 74
    on health care 66, 68
    from observation 74
reflection 48–9
relationships *see* partnerships
role-play vi
Rustin, M. 51

safety 52p
    in holding 4p, 12, 14–15
separation 14–15, 16f, 20
    apprehensions 24
    minimising 21–3, 24, 25p
    see also continuity of care
sharing 4p, 34p, 72, 74
    limitations 6–7, 51, 53
Shohet, R. 56
Shore, R. 11
sleeping 52p, 67
Smith, C. 33
Special Needs 61, 70
staff meetings 30, 38, 41, 58
Standards 37–9, 41
    clauses 60–1
    frameworks 60
    recommendations from 61–75
starting points 29, 36
statements 47, 48f
    of commitment 30–1f
    on physical closeness 54–5f
stimulation 11–12
supervision 55p, 56, 57, 58–9, 62, 71
    for child-protection policies 73
Syal, M. 14–15

team work 6, 20, 21, 39–40, 42f
    limitations 13–14
    as networks 8, 9, 13
    staff meetings 30, 38, 41, 58
terminology 19, 43f, 44
Thorpe, K 35, 48f
time 63
    limitations 30, 49–50
    paced 38, 43f, 45
training *see* continuing professional
    development
Trevarthen, C. 11–12

Vernon, J. 33

Watson, H. 58–9
Whalley, M. 57